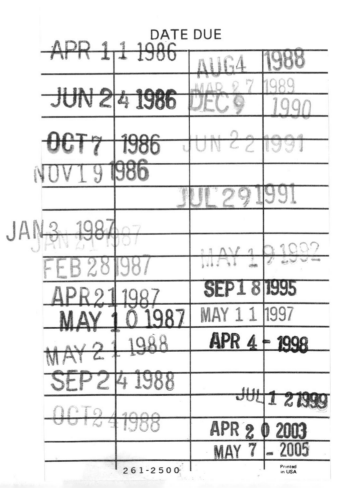

BOXEN

Lord Big

BOXEN

THE IMAGINARY WORLD OF
THE YOUNG

C. S. LEWIS

*

EDITED BY
WALTER HOOPER

Harcourt Brace Jovanovich, Publishers
San Diego   New York   London

First published in Great Britain 1985
Copyright © by C. S. Lewis Pte Ltd

Requests for permission to make copies of any part of the work should be mailed to: Permissions, Harcourt Brace Jovanovich, Publishers, Orlando, Florida 32887.

The Estate of C. S. Lewis gratefully acknowledges
The Marion E. Wade collection, Wheaton College, Illinois, USA,
for allowing the manuscripts in its possession to be photographed and Lyle W. Dorsett, its Curator, for all his help. Thanks are also due to the Rev. Walter Hooper for making available the material which he owns.

Library of Congress Catologing in Publication Data
Lewis, C. S. (Clive Staples), 1898–1963.
Boxen: the imaginary world of the young C. S. Lewis.
Summary: A collection of maps, histories, sketches, and stories created by C. S. Lewis as a child to describe his private fantasy world, known as Animal-Land or Boxen.
A scholarly introduction explains the stories in the context of Lewis's life.
1. Fantastic fiction, English. 2. Children's writings, English.
[1. Animals—Fiction. 2. Fantasy. 3. Short stories. 4. Children's writings]
I. Hooper, Walter.   II. Title
PR6023.E926B6 1985   823'.912 [Fic]   85-8478
ISBN 0-15-113630-0

Printed in the United States of America

First American edition

A B C D E

CONTENTS

INTRODUCTION

Had not Albert Lewis moved his family into 'Little Lea' on the outskirts of Belfast on the 21st April 1905 the present Little-Master of Boxen might never have been born. Albert, a police court solicitor, had the house built for his wife, Flora, and their sons. The sons were Warren, born 16th June 1895, and Clive Staples, born 29th November 1898, and they were known to their parents and friends as Warnie and Jack. Years later Jack was to say of Little Lea in Chapter I of his autobiography, *Surprised by Joy* (1955):

> To a child it seemed less like a house than a city ... The New House is almost a major character in my story. I am a product of long corridors, empty sunlit rooms, upstair indoor silences, attics explored in solitude, distant noises of gurgling cisterns and pipes, and the noise of wind under the tiles. Also, of endless books. My father bought all the books he read and never got rid of any of them. There were books in the study, books in the drawing-room, books in the cloakroom, books (two deep) in the great bookcase on the landing, books in a bedroom, books piled as high as my shoulder in the cistern attic, books of all kinds reflecting every transient stage of my parents' interests, books readable and unreadable, books suitable for a child and books most emphatically not. Nothing was forbidden me. In the seemingly endless rainy afternoons I took volume after volume from the shelves. I had always the same certainty of finding a book that was new to me as a man who walks into a field has of finding a new blade of grass ... Out of doors was 'the view' for which, no doubt, the site had principally been chosen. From our front door we looked down over wide fields to Belfast Lough and across it to the long mountain line of the Antrim shore ... This was in the far-off days when Britain was the world's carrier and the Lough was full of shipping; a delight to both us boys.

At this time it was usual for the established families of Northern Ireland to send their children to English schools. Warnie had hitherto been taught by his mother and his governess, Miss Annie Harper. Now that he was ten he had less than a month to explore Little Lea before he was sent to Wynyard School in Watford, Hertfordshire. His parents believed it to be a good school. But those who would know of the horrors that Warnie, and later Jack, found there will find a description of it in Chapter II of *Surprised by Joy* where it is called 'Belsen'. Meanwhile, Jack - for whom the parting

[7]

from Warnie was very painful – was being taught French and Latin by Mrs Lewis and everything else by Miss Harper.

Jack staked out a claim to one of the attics which became known as 'the little end room'. He found that what drove him to write was an extreme manual clumsiness owing to having only one joint in his thumbs. For this reason, and because all the desks in the house were too tall for him to write on, his parents had a table made for him. 'Jack's Desk', as it was called, is 2-feet square and 23 inches high. It was on it that the earliest stories of Animal-Land were composed, though all the Boxen stories were written in this attic room. I mention 'Jack's Desk' because of the sentimental value it always had for Jack and Warnie and because it's the only piece of furniture left from that room. Describing 'the little end room' in Chapter I of *Surprised by Joy*, Jack said:

Here my first stories were written, and illustrated, with enormous satisfaction. They were an attempt to combine my two chief literary pleasures – 'dressed animals' and 'knights-in-armour'. As a result, I wrote about chivalrous mice and rabbits who rode out in complete mail to kill not giants but cats. But already the mood of the systematiser was strong in me; the mood which led Trollope so endlessly to elaborate his Barsetshire. The Animal-Land which came into action in the holidays when my brother was at home was a modern Animal-Land; it had to have trains and steamships if it was to be a country shared with him. It followed, of course, that the medieval Animal-Land about which I wrote my stories must be the same country at an earlier period; and of course the two periods must be properly connected. This led me from romancing to historiography; I set about writing a full history of Animal-Land. Though more than one version of this instructive work is extant, I never succeeded in bringing it down to modern times; centuries take a deal of filling when all the events have to come out of the historian's head ... There was soon a map of Animal-Land – several maps, all tolerably consistent. Then Animal-Land had to be geographically related to my brother's India, and India consequently lifted out of its place in the real world. We made it an island, with its north coast running along the back of the Himalayas; between it and Animal-Land my brother rapidly invented the principal steamship routes. Soon there was a whole world and a map of that world which used every colour in my paint box. And those parts of that world which we regarded as our own – Animal-Land and India – were increasingly peopled with consistent characters.

In time Animal-Land and India were united into the single state of Boxen. Those who come to be as fond of Boxen as I am will perhaps share my regret that only a few of the earliest stories have survived. But all that has survived is in this book. Still, I dare say there will be those who will find the early writings tedious. If you are one of the latter I suggest you stop reading this and go direct to the first of what are called the 'novels' – *Boxen: Or Scenes from Boxonian City Life.*

There exist only three notebooks which contain Jack's earliest stories of Boxen, and for convenience I will call them Notebooks I, II and III. It's impossible to know exactly when any of the Boxen stories were written. However, in his incomplete *Encyclopedia Boxoniana* which Jack began in 1927, he mentions *The King's Ring* as 'almost certainly the oldest text'. Considering the position of this story in Notebook I and comparing it to some things I know to have been written in 1907, I'm fairly certain that *The King's Ring* was written quite early in 1906. The adventures of Sir Peter Mouse in *Manx Against Manx* and *The Relief of Murry* provide an illustration of the shift from modern to medieval. They come from Notebook I and were possibly written in 1906.

King Bunny – or King Benjamin I – is one of the Boxen characters inspired by a toy. The interest in 'knights-in-armour' came from, amongst other sources, Sir Arthur Conan Doyle's *Sir Nigel* which was serialised in *The Strand Magazine* from December 1905 to December 1906. Much of the vocabulary of *The King's Ring* – such as 'gossip' for 'friend' – and the decision to make it a play were almost certainly in imitation of Shakespeare. In Notebook I Jack scribbled, 'Who do you think wrote the best plays? I can form a good idea which poet wrote the best. When Shakespeare was alive he wrote the best, what play do you think was the best. I think *Hamlet* was.'

The years 1906–1907 were particularly happy for the Lewis family. Warnie had good reasons for disliking Wynyard School, but he was as delighted as anyone with Little Lea. In his letters to Jack he urged him to see that a cricket pitch was made in the garden. And Jack, for his part, kept Warnie abreast of the developments in Boxen. Many years later Warnie arranged the family papers into chronological order and typed them. When it was all finished, they were bound into eleven volumes and given the name *Lewis Papers: Memoirs of the Lewis Family 1850–1930.* It is from the *Lewis Papers* that I've drawn much of my information about Boxen and I've preserved the original spelling from Jack and Warnie's letters. Jack had an unfortunate habit of not dating his, but in one to Warnie which was prob-

ably written in September 1906 he said: 'At present Boxen is *slightly* con-
vulsed. The news had just reached her that King Bunny is a prisoner. The
colonists (who are of course the war party) are in a bad way: they dare
scarcely leave their houses because of the mobs. In Tararo the Prussians
and Boxonians are at fearful odds against each other and the natives. Such
were the states of affairs recently: but the able general Quicksteppe is taking
steps for the rescue of King Bunny. (The news somewhat pacified the
rioters.)'[1] For years there had been rumours of a possible war with Prussia,
and it was natural that if King Benjamin I was to have enemies they might
as well be the ones Jack heard so much about.

Readers of C.S. Lewis's seven Chronicles of Narnia will know that after
writing *The Lion, the Witch and the Wardrobe* and the next four stories, he
turned back to seek the origins of Narnia. Having found them, they were
described in *The Magician's Nephew*. Much the same happened with Boxen.
Was anyone in Animal-Land before the reign of Benjamin I? How did they
get to know the people of India? In a letter to Warnie of about June 1907
Jack said: 'I am thinking of writeing a History of Mouse-land and I have
even gon so far as to make up some of it, this is what I have made up.
Mouse-land had a very long stone-age during which time no great things
tooke place it lasted from 55 BC to 1212 and then king Bublich I began to
reign, he was not a good king but he fought gainest yellow land. Bub II his
son fought indai about the lantern act, died 1377 king Bunny came next.'[2]

The *History of Mouse-Land from Stone-Age to Bublish I*, published here
from Notebook II does not go as far as the 'lantern act'. Even so, I think
this is probably the history which Jack was outlining. The other histories
mentioned in the *Encyclopedia* are lost with the exception of what is about
the first half of the one Jack considered the best. It is named in the *Encyclopedia* as the *New History* or the *History of Animal-Land*, and the story of
how it survived is a pleasant little piece of earthly history. In 1953 Jack
Lewis's friend Lord David Cecil revealed that his eleven year-old son, Hugh,
would be grateful if Jack would read the history of his invented world. Such
was his pleasure in Hugh's work that he lent him the *History of Animal-
Land*. Fortunately, Hugh copied down as much of this history as he could
before the manuscript had to be returned. He cannot regret more than I do

[1] *Lewis Papers*, vol. III, p. 76. The original of the *Lewis Papers* is in Wheaton College, Wheaton,
Illinois, and there is a copy in the Bodleian Library, Oxford.
[2] *Ibid.*, p. 80.

that there was not time to transcribe it all. But because of Hugh Cecil much that we could never have known about Animal-Land is preserved.

A peculiarity of Mr Lewis's was that he disliked intensely going on holidays and he usually pleaded pressure of work in order to avoid leaving Belfast. Mrs Lewis, on the other hand, enjoyed travelling and during September 1907 she took Jack and Warnie for a holiday in France. Writing to his father on the 4th September, Warnie said: 'Jacks started a new book "Living races of Mouse-land" which will be very good *when* it is finished.'[1] In emphasising '*when*' Warnie meant that Jack often began stories which he never completed. There is much evidence of this in the Notebooks, but this is what you would expect of one gifted with such a lively and fertile imagination. When, as in this case, so many of the completed stories have vanished fragments often supply needed illumination. In Chapter IV of *The Locked Door* that most prominent of Frogs, Lord Big, honours Little-Master White from the island of Piscia as 'the greatest Little-Master ever seen by Boxen'. It occurs to me that the following fragment from Notebook II entitled *Life of Little Mr White* may have been the first thing written about Little-Master White and Piscia. And is it not likely that the combination of 'Little' and 'Mr' suggested to Jack the title of 'Little-Master'? The fragment says:

White as we know is of good qualitys as a frog, but strange to say is of poor lineage. Many people are under an error concerning his family history. He can be traced to the Bigs. His derect parents were farmers in the country of Frog-land, but his grand-father was the brother of Big's father: thus Marshel Wite is conected with the famous Sir Big but was much younger. Mr Little was borne at slimey-bay in the reign of 'King Mouse the Good'. Wite at the age of 10 left his school, and served Tom Anderson for 13 years. (Tom Anderson was a millar.) No sooner had he left Tom Anderson than he went into the Army.

During the Christmas holidays of 1907 Jack began the first of his diaries. Or, more accurately, his first autobiography as it bears the title *My Life*. As this happy family was soon to be shattered, Jack's *Life* gives us a glimpse of what it was like at Little Lea before it changed so much. The servants at Little Lea included a house-maid named Maude Scott and a cook named Martha or 'Mat'. Jack intended that the *Life* should be read by all in the

[1] *Ibid.*, p. 82.

house and it is dedicated 'To Miss Maude Scott'. That was to prove very embarrassing because in the first paragraph he states: 'I have a lot of eny-mays, however there are only 2 in this house they are called Maude and Mat, Maude is far worse than Mat, but she thinks she is a saint ... I HATE Maude.' He goes on to say: 'Papy of course is the master of the house, and a man in whom you can see strong Lewis features, bad temper, very sensible, nice wen not in a temper. Mamy is like most middle-aged ladys, stout, brown hair, spectaciles, kniting her chief industry etc. etc. I am like most boys of 9 and I am like Papy, bad temper, thick lips, thin and generally wearing a jersey.' After describing his pets (a mouse, a canary and a dog) he mentions his paternal grandfather: 'I have left out an important member of the family namly my grand-father, who lives in a little room of his own up-stairs he is a nice old man in some ways but he pitys him-self rather much, however all old people do that.'

So great was his affection for Warnie that there is a section of the *Life* entitled 'Part IV. How Warnie came home.' As, however, Warnie had not yet arrived from Wynyard, Jack went on to write: 'I am still looking forward to Warnie's homecoming which is always a great event in our house. You see I had to wait for something to happen before I could write about it, and I put down "Part IV" "How Warnie came home" with out thinking ... therefore I shall have to fill up "Part IV" with other things. I have yet left out another important person who plays a large part in "my life", namely "Miss Harper" who is my governess. She is fairly nice FOR a governess, but all of them are the same. Miss Harper has fair hair, blue eyes, and rather sharp features, she generally wears a green blouse and a dress of the same hue.' Included in the *Life* was a drawing of Miss Harper with a 'balloon' coming from her lips which contained the words 'Don't say can't to me, Jacksie.'[1]

Miss Harper, a Presbyterian of a rather serious disposition, almost certainly read the *Life*. By way of an answer, she wrote in Notebook I a strongly-worded discourse on 'Do as you would be done by.' That arrow apparently found its target. Notebook II overlaps with number I and Jack scribbled in it, 'I often wish that I was leading a more use-ful life.'

In 1908 Mrs Lewis began to feel ill. When she was operated on at Little Lea on the 15th February she was discovered to have cancer. For a while she seemed better. But it didn't last and this brave lady died on the 23rd

[1] *Ibid.*, pp. 88-91.

August 1908. Perhaps her virtues and her character are no where better summed up than in the first chapter of *Surprised by Joy*: 'With my mother's death all settled happiness, all that was tranquil and reliable, disappeared from my life. There was to be much fun, many pleasures, many stabs of Joy, but no more of the old security. It was sea and islands now; the great continent had sunk like Atlantis.'

Less than a month after their mother's death Jack became Warnie's fellow sufferer at Wynyard. They had no more idea than their parents that the Headmaster, Robert Capron, was insane. Besides his cruelty, it disappointed Jack that Capron's teaching consisted of little more than 'a shoreless ocean of arithmetic'. Years later, when I was Jack's private secretary, he gave me Notebooks I and III – the first because it contained his first story of Animal-Land and the other because it was one of those he used at Wynyard for his prep. 'Look at all that arithmetic!' he said to me. 'But,' said I, 'isn't that algebra?' 'Is it?' he exclaimed. 'Then it was a shoreless ocean of arithemetic *and algebra*!'

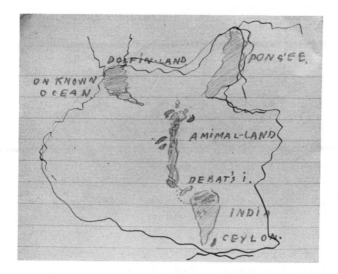

During the Christmas holiday of 1908 Jack added considerably to Boxen. In Notebook II there is what was possibly the first map of Animal-Land and the other parts of that world. India is situated south of Animal-Land with Ceylon where it is in the real world. North of Animal-Land is Dolfin-Land and on the same latitude and east of Dolfin-Land is Pongee.

Running through both these countries is the 'Arctic Circle' beyond which lies a vast expanse of 'Unexplored Ice'. Also in Notebook II is Part I of *The Chess Monograph*. Part II is taken from Notebook III which Jack apparently overlooked when he was compiling his *Encyclopedia*. India had been discovered to be an inconvenient distance from Animal-Land and in the map drawn to go with *The Geography of Animal-Land*, in Notebook III, India has been pulled up so as to lie east of Animal-Land with the island of Piscia (formerly Frog-Land) in between.

It was during their year together at Wynyard that Warnie began a Boxonian newspaper, and while no issues have survived, it was probably during 1908-1909 that Jack's *The Murry Chronicle* and *The Murry Evening Telegraph* began 'publication'. And with the newspapers came some of Jack's most detailed drawings of such notables as Lord Big, Viscount Puddiphat and James Bar. Excepting those pictures which were drawn *in* the 'novels', some of the best illustrations were drawn on loose sheets of paper and collected in 1926 into the two volumes of *Leborough Studies*. As most are dated as having been drawn between 1908-1910 it would seem that these years formed a high point in Boxen's creation. The pity is that we don't have the stories the drawings were intended to illustrate.

Warnie won his freedom from Wynyard after the summer term of 1909 and in September of that year he entered Malvern College. Deprived of his fellow Boxen enthusiast, Jack began a 'medieval' novel entitled *The Ajimywanian War*. After the friendly dressed animals of Boxen, what he wrote of this story in which all the characters are human is unexpectedly dull. It was copied into the *Lewis Papers* (vol. III, pp. 162-164). About the same time he created a series of small territories around the 'Ilonian Sea'. The fragment of the story, with a detailed map, about these far-eastern territories is found in Notebook III. But it contains none of the delights of Boxen, and this may explain why it never got very far. But these inventions, while totally un-Boxonian in character, found a small place in Boxen. The country in which the Ajimywanian War took place was Ojimywania and the only map we have of Clarendon (which is in the 'South Seas' and west of Tararo) is called 'Clarendon *or* Ojimywania' One of the territories bordering the Ilonian Sea is Gleonarphy. Although it sounds like a desert, it must have been perfect for growing tobacco. When, in *Littera Scripta Manet* ('The Written Word Abides'), Lord Big offers General Quicksteppe one of his best cigars (kept in a safe) it is 'one of the Gleonarphies'.

In April 1910 Robert Capron wrote to Mr Lewis to say that he was 'giving up school work'. And when Jack arrived home in July Mr Lewis decided that until another English school could be found for him he would be sent to Campbell College in Belfast for the autumn term. However, when Jack came home from Campbell on Sunday the 13th November he had such a fearful cough that the doctor advised a complete rest. Since their mother died Mr Lewis had written weekly letters to his sons. His loathing of travel prevented him from visiting them at Wynyard, but in other respects he was both father and mother to his sons whom he loved dearly. Jack spoke of the two months he was to spend at home as a time when he and his father 'were famously snug together'. It was never to be so 'tranquil and reliable' as when Mrs Lewis was alive. But love flowed from many family members. No one could have been better to Jack and Warnie than their mother's cousins Sir William and Lady Ewart and their three grown daughters who lived at Glenmachan House (called 'Mountbracken' in *Surprised by Joy*). Glenmachan was a second home to them. When I read of that grand ball in *The Locked Door* in which Lord Big dances with the Duchess of Penzley I am reminded of the beautiful ball room at Glenmachan House which I saw while there were still members of the Ewart family there.

But it wasn't that gracious home that Jack had in mind when in Chapter III of *Surprised by Joy* he describes those dances, really for adults, to which friends of his father felt obliged to invite him. After complaining about the 'discomfort of one's Eton suit and stiff shirt' and 'prancing about on a polished floor till the small hours of the morning' he says 'I positively felt that I could have torn my hostess limb from limb. Why should she pester me? I had never done her any harm, never asked *her* to a party.' Had it not been for those Belfast hostesses I wonder if the dances at Boxen's Riverside Palace could be half so amusing as they are. But when Lord Big announces in *Littera Scripta Manet* that 'my dancing days are over' he speaks for Jack as much as for himself.

More serious to Jack, in bringing Boxen up to modern times, was what to do about the clothes of that time, so heavily starched as to be almost bullet-proof. He had been considering the problem for several years and it is summed up in a little treatise from Notebook II on *How to Make Man Picturesc*:

In his present state it is all-most impossible to do such a a thing. For instance: 'The hideous topper', 'The Loathsome frock coat.' Ouf the beastly things, how can man continue to wear them? The dress in which boys are generally clothed are not much better. The sailor suit is awful!! Terrible! FEARFUL!! The thing is that some old-fashioned dress must be adopted, and I really think that *then* man might look picturesc.

Mr Lewis was able to find a place for Jack at Cherbourg House, the preparatory school which overlooked Malvern College. This meant that the brothers were to be within half a mile of one another and they set out for Cherbourg and Malvern (called 'Chartres' and 'Wyvern' in *Surprised by Joy*) in January 1911. It was to prove a success with Jack, and he was to be there until July 1913 when he won a scholarship to Malvern College.

In a letter to Jack of the 29th January 1911, Mr Lewis said: 'I went to the Hippodrome last night to see if it would raise the internal barometer a degree or two.'[1] Mr Lewis always found his 'internal barometer' raised by the vaudeville of the Belfast Hippodrome and the Empire Theatre and it was something he liked to enjoy with his sons. Writing about those visits to the Hippodrome, Jack said in Chapter IV of *Surprised by Joy*:

> My father ... often of a Saturday night would take us to the Belfast Hippodrome. I recognise now that I never had the taste for vaudeville which he shared with my brother. At the time I supposed myself to be enjoying the show, but I was mistaken ... What I enjoyed was merely the etcetera of the show, the bustle and lights, the sense of having a night out, the good spirits of my father in his holiday mood, and – above all – the admirable cold supper to which we came back at about ten o'clock.

A very different kind of enthusiast of the theatre was a young master Jack fell under the spell of at Cherbourg. In his description of 'Pogo' (the master) in that same chapter of his autobiography, Jack wrote:

> Pogo was a wit, Pogo was a dressy man, Pogo was a man about town ... Pogo was a great theatrical authority. We soon knew all the latest songs. We soon knew all about the famous actresses of that age – Lily Elsie, Gertie Millar, Zena Dare. Pogo was a fund of information about their private lives. We learned from him all the latest jokes; where we did not understand he was ready to give us help. He explained many things. After a term of Pogo's society one had the feeling of being not twelve weeks but twelve years older.

I first read the Boxen 'novels' during that part of 1963 when I was Jack's secretary and living in his home in Oxford. When he discovered how charmed I was by the sartorial splendour of Viscount Puddiphat (the owner

[1] *Ibid.*, p. 227.

of many 'Alhambra' music-halls) he drew my attention to the two passages quoted above. We also talked about the absorption by so many Boxonians with politics, which he said came directly from his father and his father's friends. But the political side of Boxen life is no where so clearly explained than in the excellent Memoir which Warnie wrote to go with his edition of *Letters of C.S. Lewis* (1966) and in which he said:

> In the upper-middle-class society of our Belfast childhood, politics and money were the chief, almost the only subjects of grown-up conversation: and since no visitors came to our house who did not hold precisely the same political views as my father, what we heard was not discussion and the lively clash of minds, but rather an endless and one-sided torrent of grumble and vituperation. Any ordinary parent would have sent us boys off to amuse ourselves, but not my father: we had to sit in silence and endure it. The immediate result, in Jack's case, was to convince him that grown-up conversation and politics were one and the same thing, and that everything he wrote must therefore be given a political framework: the long-term result was to fill him with a disgust and revulsion from the very idea of politics before he was out of his 'teens.

When Jack spoke of himself in his *Life* as having his father's 'bad temper' he almost certainly meant that he shared his father's gift for oratory. Describing this aspect of Mr Lewis in Chapter II of *Surprised by Joy* he said: 'He . . . relied wholly on his tongue as the instrument of domestic discipline . . . When he opened his mouth to reprove us he no doubt intended a short well-chosen appeal to our common sense and conscience. But alas, he had been a public speaker long before he became a father. He had for many years been a public prosecutor. Words came to him and intoxicated him as they came.' Jack realised that anyone who happened to read about the almost despotic hold Lord Big has over King Benjamin VII and Rajah Hawki V would suppose Lord Big to be a portrait of Mr Lewis. 'The reader', he says in Chapter V of his autobiography

> will divine a certain resemblance between the life of the two kings under Lord Big and our own life under our father. He will be right. But Big was not, in origin, simply our Father first batrachised and then caricatured in some directions and glorified in others. He was in many ways a prophetic portrait of Sir Winston Churchill as Sir Winston Churchill came to be during the last war . . . The two soverigns who allowed themselves to be dominated by Lord Big were King Benjamin VIII of Animal-Land and Rajah Hawki (I think, VI) of India. They had much in common with my brother and myself. But their fathers, the elder Benjamin and the elder Hawki, had not. The Fifth Hawki is a shadowy figure; but the Seventh Benjamin (a rabbit, as you will have guessed)

is a rounded character. I can see him still – the heaviest-jowled and squarest-builded of all rabbits, very fat in his later years ... His earlier life had been dominated by the belief that he could be both a king and an amateur detective. He never succeeded in the later role, partly because the chief enemy whom he was pursuing (Mr Baddlesmere) was not really a criminal at all but a lunatic – a complication which would have thrown out the plans of Sherlock Holmes himself. But he very often got himself kidnapped ... Once, on his return from such a misadventure, he had dyed him and the familiar brown figure re-appeared as a piebald rabbit ... The judgement of history cannot pronounce him either a good rabbit or a good King; but he was not a nonentity. He ate prodigiously.

Jack Lewis probably never imagined that these stories would be published. And he was only having some fun when he said in his *Encyclopedia* that certain problems must be left to 'the future Boxonologist'. Honoured as I am in being appointed to edit the stories I suppose my old friend would, with his usual gaiety, call me that future Boxonologist. He might even have suggested me as the first holder of the Lord Big Chair of Boxonology. If so, then I think the inventor of Boxen would regard it as my duty to point out that the monarchs 'dominated' by Lord Big were Benjamin VII and Hawki V. There has not yet been a Benjamin VIII and a Hawki VI. A far more painful duty is to report that none of the stories of the *Sixth* Benjamin who pursued Mr Baddlesmere exist. Nevertheless, the stories which have survived are too many in number if this book is not going to be too expensive for most readers. For this reason I have not included in it the fragment *Tararo*, *The Life of Lord John Big* and *Littera Scripta Manet*. But those stories will be most tenderly preserved, and I hope to publish them when the time is right for a second volume of Boxen stories.

As already mentioned, none of these stories can be dated exactly. Even Jack could not help me with this. He did, however, say that he thought the series came to an end before he entered Malvern College. Warnie also seemed to think they had all been written before the autumn of 1913. However, a few years before Warnie died he scribbled some possible dates on the novels. On the cover of *Boxen* he wrote, 'Obviously written in 1912 – see p. 26.' What is on that page is an invitation from one of the characters which is dated April 3rd 1912. Warnie attempted to date the other novels by this same kind of 'internal evidence' – the years mentioned *in* the stories. Considering how much the handwriting changes from the first to the last of the novels and, even more, the quality of the writing, I think it unlikely that all were written in little more than a twelvemonth. The dates which appear *within* the stories could be as much a part of the invention as everything else. It seems unlikely that within a year Jack could, in his *Life of Lord John Big*, forget that Lord Big was created Little-Master before the expedition to the Tracity Island and not afterwards. My guess is that the first of the novels, *Boxen*, could have been written as far back as Christmas 1910.

Jack seldom re-read any of his published works. There is, however, much to suggest that of all he wrote, published and unpublished, it was the Boxen stories that he and Warnie read most often. It was a door into one of the most pleasant parts of their lives. We can't know Boxen as they did. Even so, the remarkable thing is the amount of pleasure to which we are admitted. When I first read *The Iliad* as a boy and knew nothing about Homer I could not have guessed whether Homer was 'for' the Greeks against the Trojans or whether it was the other way round. And when I knew more about Homer it did nothing to change what I most like about *The Iliad*: the writer's admiration and good will towards everyone and even every *thing* that is truly good in its way. So with Boxen. One would expect the young boy to make much of those steam ships and railways which he naturally liked. But what of those stupefying conversations about politics? By being dipped in his imagination the things he disliked in the real world became as much as anything a part of a single, delightful whole. The characters and their doings have their individual excellences, and nothing is despised. Finally, when the grown-up C.S. Lewis re-read the stories in preparation for beginning his *Encyclopedia*, he wrote to his brother saying, 'I suppose it is only accident, but it is hard to resist the convictions that one is dealing with a sort of reality.' Perhaps he was. Perhaps we are too.

Oxford WALTER HOOPER
23 May 1984

Colonel Chutney and Lt James Bar in the
stokehold of the yacht *Cygnet*

THE BOXEN MANUSCRIPTS

C.S. 'Jack' Lewis wrote what there is of his *Encyclopedia Boxoniana* on visits to his father's house, Little Lea in Belfast, in September 1927 and in April 1928. Albert Lewis died on the 25th September 1929 and as Jack had a home in Oxford and as Warnie was in the Army they decided to sell Little Lea. On their last day there, the 23rd April 1930, they arranged to transfer all the Boxen manuscripts to Oxford. The trunk containing all the toys which had served as models for various Boxen characters was buried in the garden of the house.

I think one of the reasons why Jack did not complete his *Encyclopedia* is because, in turning out the contents of his father's house, he came across many Boxen manuscripts previously overlooked. The fragment to which I have given the name *Tararo* is one of the manuscripts found after Albert Lewis died. Jack told me that when he was writing about his invented world in *Surprised by Joy* he had in front of him many Boxen stories and maps which had come to light after his father's death. Indeed, I saw a great many of them when I was his secretary. When Jack and his brother wrote to one another about the stories they referred to the longer works or 'novels' as the 'ones we usually read'. They are the ones I read when living in Jack's home, The Kilns, in Headington Quarry, Oxford.

Jack and Warnie had been living at The Kilns since 1930. Then, when Jack died on the 22nd November 1963, Warnie was afraid he could not afford to go on living there and he decided to move into a smaller house. Preparatory to his moving into the smaller place where I was to join him, I was living in Keble College with Dr and Mrs Austin Farrer. One day in January 1964 I went out to see Warnie. I discovered from the gardener, Paxford, that Warnie has been burning various papers on a bonfire for the last three days. That day Paxford had been instructed to put on the bonfire a good many notebooks and papers which he recognised as being in the handwriting of C.S. Lewis. He knew that I would wish to preserve them and when he mentioned this to Warnie he was told that if I appeared that day I could have them. Otherwise they were to be burned. And so it was that I arrived in time to save many things from the flames. Amongst the papers given me by Warnie was what in the Introduction I've called Notebook II, the exercise book containing the *Encyclopedia* and a number of Boxen maps.

Not long after this Warnie said in his Memoir to *Letters of C.S. Lewis* (1966) that 'After [Jack's] death, we found among his papers any number of childish but ambitious beginnings of histories, stories, poems, nearly all of them dealing with our private fantasy world of Animal-Land or Boxen.' Except for the two notebooks given me by Jack and those few items saved from the fire, what Warnie saved were those 'novels' which range from *Boxen* to *Littera Scripta Manet* and the two volumes of family drawings called *Leborough Studies Ranging from 1905-1916*, a number of which drawings appear in this book. He was very fond of these and before he died on the 9th April 1973 he arranged for all of them to go to the Marion E. Wade Collection at Wheaton College in Wheaton, Illinois. At some time before Warnie died those pages in the second volume of the *Leborough Studies* which contained the first act of the *Unfinished Play* (mentioned in Jack's *Encyclopedia*) had been torn out. It is not known when this happened or why.

I am grateful that Professor Lyle Dorsett of the Marion E. Wade Collection allowed the Lewis Estate to photograph the illustrations from the Boxen 'novels' and the drawings by C.S. Lewis contained in the *Leborough Studies*. There are facsimile copies of those Boxen manuscripts owned by Wheaton College in the Bodleian Library.

W.H.

ANIMAL-LAND

DRAMATIS PERSONÆ

SIR PETER-MOUSE " " " knight in waiting on king.

BUNNY " " " " king of animal-land

ic-THIS-OBESS " son to Deab bagher, singer

TOM-MOUSE }
BOB-MOUSE } " " " sons to icthus-oress.

TOM-MOUSE " " " " a spinner

BOB-MOUSE " " " " a priest

Mᴮ GOLD-FISH " " generel to king

SIR-BIG " " " a frog fielding-ohel

GOLLYOG " " " " his servant

SIR-GOOSE " " rich baron & spy

DORIMIE " " " " " a page

HIT " " " " " a thief

BROWNIE-BAND.

Mᴮ BLUE " " " " conducter.

Mᴮ YELLOW " " " " " drumer.

Mᴮ J. MAUVE " " " " trumpeter

Mᴮ B. MAUVE " " " " bugler.

Mᴮ READ " " " clappers.

———

HARBOUR-MASTER'S JUGD'S SAILORS ETC.

THE KING'S RING

(*A Comedy*)

Interesting carictars. Famous ones. For instance, Sir Big, a world-famed gentleman. A very good choreus and nice scenry. (Slight comic tints in and out threw it.[1])

PREFACE

The play was ment to take place in the year 1327 the reign of King Bunny Ist. Befor his reign the country was called Bublish and was under the rule of King Bublish. It was in their to reigns that Mr Icthus-oress made his fortune by playing the harp; he got his name from fighting an Ichthus-oress; his father a butcher died 1307.

Dramatis Personae

SIR PETER MOUSE	Kinight in waiting on King
BUNNY	King of Animal-land
ICTHUS-ORESS	Son to dead butcher, singer
TOM MOUSE ⎱ *sons to Icthus-oress*	A spinner
BOB MOUSE ⎰	A priest
MR GOLD FISH	General to King
SIR BIG	A frog fieldmarshel
GOLLYWOG	His servant
SIR GOOSE	Rich baron, spy
DORIMIE	A page
HIT	A thief

---

[1] For instance ... 'But it dos not please me.' Act 3, Scene I

[25]

Brownie Band

MR BLUE	Conducter
MR YELLOW	Drummer
MR J. MAUVE	Trumpeter
MR B. MAUVE	Bugleur
MR READ	Clappers

Judges, Harbour-Masters, Sailors etc.

Places

PIP CASTLE is King Bunny's palace
MURRY, a town in Mouse-Land
MOURN HILLS, hills at back of Murry
MOUSE LANE, road between Pip Castle and Murry
THE GOOSE INN, an inn in Murry
JEMIMA, a river on which Murry is built
TOPSY, a port at mouth of Jemima
CANNON-TOWN, a city in Rabbit-Land

ACT I

Scene I: The Goose Inn.
(KING BUNNY *and* PETER MOUSE *discouvered drinking.*
BAR-MAN *behind counter.*)

KING BUNNY: This wine is good.
BAR-MAN: I shall drink a stiff goblet to the health of King Bunny.
KING BUNNY: For this good toast much thanks.
SIR PETER: Draws near the dinner hour so pleas your Magasty.
KING BUNNY: Run go bid the kooks to wait. (*Exit* SIR PETER.)
BAR-MAN: How now your Magasty. The clock strikes one.
KING BUNNY: I wager you my shoe that I shall put you home. Is that what you mean?
BAR-MAN: Yes I do mean it.
   (*Curtain.*)

Scene II: A room in Pip Castle. (SIR BIG, GOLLYWOG, etc., KING BUNNY, SIR PETER etc. *eating dinner*.)

SIR PETER: (*to* KING BUNNY) Know you the bar-man's name?

KING BUNNY: His name is Hit.

GOLD FISH: T'is an odd one in sooth, how came you know it your Magasty?

KING BUNNY: I heard folk call him Hit. (*Enter a* SERVANT.)

SERVANT: A Mouse stands at the gate and he would speak with your Magasty.

SIR BIG
KING BUNNY } Let him come.
SIR PETER

    (*Exit* SERVANT.)

SIR PETER: Who might it be? What might he want?

    (*Re-enter* SERVANT *with* HIT.)

SERVANT: This is the Mouse.

KING BUNNY: How-now good Hit.

HIT: I am well. I hope I find the same. How tight thy ring is.

(KING BUNNY *tacks it of. Goes to window to look at mark on finger*.)

HIT: (*aside*) I am a lucky Mouse.

    (*Tacks ring. Exit*.)

KING BUNNY: (*turns*) O where is my ring and where is Hit?

    (*Curtain*.)

Scene III: Mr Ichus-oress's House.
(MR ICTHUS-ORESS, BOB, TOM and GOLLIWOG.)

MR ICTHUS-ORESS: Wilt have a game of cards?

GOLLYWOG ⎫
         ⎬ Yes
TOM   ⎭

BOB: The law of mine order allows me not such idle pleasures.

MR ICTHUS-ORESS: Thou needst not play, then.

   (*Enter* SIR PETER MOUSE.)

SIR PETER: Hast sceene the King's ring? T'is lost.

MR ICTHUS-ORESS: Lost!! None of us saw it.

SIR PETER: It must be found.

   (*Exit.*)

MR ICTHUS-ORESS: T'is bad.

BOB: May wee be saved from the theft that stole King Bunny's ring.

TOM: Thy bald and brainless pate shall do no good.

MR ICTHUS-ORESS: Hush I hear footsteps.

   (*Enter* HIT *bearing* BUNNY'S *ring made to look like a common ring.*)

HIT: I'll sell you ring for one Ducat.

MR ICTHUS-ORESS: (*gives ducat*) I shall buy it.

   (*Curtain.*)

ACT II

Scene I: Murry. SIR BIG's house.

(Enter SIR BIG, SIR PETER, GOLLYWOG, *etc.)*

SIR BIG: Gollywog.

GOLLYWOG: My lord.

SIR BIG: Get me mine aurmer. I and the good Sir Peter mean to find the king's ring.

(Exit GOLLYWOG.*)*

SIR PETER: Wee set our selves to a hard task.

SIR BIG: Indeed wee do sir.

(Enter MR BLUE.*)*

MR BLUE: I too shall help to find the king's ring.

(Exit all. Enter MR ICTHUS-ORESS, TOM, BOB, GOLLYWOG.*)*

MR ICTHUS-ORESS: The ring which I have bought is good.

TOM: How goes the story of Bun's ring I wonder.

(Enter MR BLUE *with arrow in his side borne by* MR YELLOW.*)*

MR BLUE: I asked Mr Hit had he got it[1] but he got angry and shot an arrow at me.

MᴮIC 'hushe I hear footsteps'

[1] 'It' means ring.

MR ICTHUS-ORESS: He is a false knave.

TOM⎫
BOB⎭ In sooth.

(*Enter the rest of* BROWNIE BAND *and* DORIMIE.)
DORIMIE: (*to* MR BLUE) I have revenged you.
MR BLUE: Much thank for that.
  (*Curtain.*)

Scene II: A boat. SIR BIG'S cabin.
(*Flourish. Enter* SIR PETER, GOLLYWOG *and* DORIMIE.)

SIR BIG: O now we sail to Cannon-Town for there that false knave Hit has
  fled. Wee mean punish him for shooting at Mr Blue.
SIR PETER: Indeed you speak sooth. Ho!! Dorimie.
DORIMIE: My lord.
SIR PETER: Get me some wine.
  (*Exit all. Flourish. Enter* MR ICTHUS-ORESS.)
MR ICTHUS-ORESS: (*sings*)
                Something ti tack a tack to
                Hurting the feelings of you.
  (*Enter* HIT.)
HIT: Hail gossip. Dist like the ring I gave thee.
MR ICTHUS-ORESS: O verry well.
  (*Curtain.*)

Scene III: The Liberry at Cannon-Town.
(*Enter a* HERALD. *At last* SIR BIG, SIR PETER, MR GOLD FISH
and all the BROWNIE BAND, MR BLUE *included.*)

HERALD: Be it now told that Archaabald Hit hath been made a member of the order of knight. Ye reason why be not told ye public.
(*Exit* HERALD: *Flourish. Enter* KING BUNNY *followed by* DORIMIE.)
KING BUNNY: Come hither friends and list to me. I knighted Hit to draw him near me, for the nearer he is to me the more I know about him.
ALL: Yes, well.
KING BUNNY: Don't you know that we have thought from the first that Hit had stolen my ring? And so I mean to see if he realy has.
MR BLUE: I, Sir Big, and Sir Peter Mouse, intend to find thy ring but we heard that Hit had come hither.
KING BUNNY: O I see.
(*Curtain.*)

ACT III

Scene I: A public garden in Cannon-Town.
(DORIMIE *and* MR ICTHUS-ORESS *discovered.*)

DORIMIE: Hail.
MR ICTHUS-ORESS: Good-day sir.
DORIMIE: The same to you gossip.
MR ICTHUS-ORESS: The day is fine.
DORIMIE: Indeed it is good man.
MR ICTHUS-ORESS: Nice gardens.
DORIMIE: Look hear minstrel.
MR ICTHUS-ORESS: Yes.
DORIMIE: I want you to teach me to sing.
MR ICTHUS-ORESS: All right, this the way I sing (*sings*)
                          the owl and the
                          pussy cat went to sea.
DORIMIE: To see what?
MR ICTHUS-ORESS: To the sea.
DORIMIE: O, was it the see of, what Bishop?

(*Enter* SIR BIG.)

SIR BIG: In sooth thou hast a nice ring.

MR ICTHUS-ORESS: Yes.

SIR BIG: (*suddenly finding it is* BUNNY'S *ring*) How is this? This is King Bunny's ring made up to look like a comon one, at last I have found the theif ho!! Mr Blue, Sir Peter Mouse, Gollywog, I've got the King's ring.
(*Enter* SIR PETER MOUSE, GOLLYWOG *and* MR BLUE.)

MR BLUE: Hail Big, what means this noise?

GOLLYWOG: T'is strange.

SIR PETER: O what means this? Explain thy-selfe my lord Sir Big.

DORIMIE: Give him time.

MR BLUE: Be silent page.

SIR BIG: (*points to* MR ICTHUS-ORESS) On him. On the theif.

SIR PETER: Who!! Which!! Where!! When!! Why!! What!! How!!

SIR BIG: Take hold good freinds and listin, seeing all the while that he does not run away.

SIR PETER
GOLLYWOG } Yes.
MR BLUE

SIR BIG: What no answer Dorimie, in the name of the king cach hold!!
(*Enter* SIR GOOSE.)

DORIMIE: But my lord Big, Mr Icthus-oress was my freind –

SIR GOOSE: (*inturupting*) Hush o hush, good Sir Big. I can give thee the true history of the king's ring.

MR ICTHUS-ORESS: And so can I.

SIR BIG: Hold thy tounge theif. Go on Goose, what is the history of the ring.

SIR GOOSE: That Hit tooke it that time when good King Bunny had it off and then Hit made it up to look like a comon ring and soled it to Mr Icthus-oress, but Icthus-oress did not know it was Bunny's ring so you can not blame him, but why has all this fuss been made King Bunny could have got a new one which would have been as good.

SIR PETER } Ah but this ring was an air-loom.
SIR BIG

SIR GOOSE: O I see.

MR ICTHUS-ORESS: But we will have to punich Hit for 2 things. I. – stealing Bunny's ring. 2. – geting me in to trouble.

[32]

MR BLUE
SIR PETER
SIR BIG
SIR GOOSE } Yes

(*Exit all but* SIR GOOSE.)

SIR GOOSE: And now I'm all alone. I am not a natif of this country realy. I'm a spy and I have been spying all the time. Thats how I knew about the ring.

(*Enter* DORIMIE.)

DORIMIE: A man wants to speak to you so please you sir.

SIR GOOSE: But it dos not please me. What is his name?

DORIMIE: Hit.

SIR GOOSE: O let him come.

(*Exit* DORIMIE.)

SIR GOOSE: Ah now I've got *him* in my power. *Him* no less ho ho ho ha ha ha he he he hi hi hi. (*goes and looks down a walk behind a bank*) O now he [is] coming. Thats him is it not? (*in a lowe voice*) O come on Hit never to go back in freedom. (*enter* HIT) Hail good Hit.

HIT: Hail.

SIR GOOSE: Ah now you'll walke off my prisoner.

(*Exit* SIR GOOSE *draging* HIT. *Curtain.*)

Scene II: Cannon-Town. The Town Hall.

(*Enter* KING BUNNY, SIR PETER MOUSE, MR GOLD FISH, SIR BIG, MR BLUE, SIR GOOSE *and* DORIMIE.)

KING BUNNY: Ah now I want to know if any one in this town hall can tell me the true history of my ring and whats still more importent give it back to me. But come I have been told that some one named Sir Goose knows it. Is he there?

SIR GOOSE: Yes here my lord.

KING BUNNY: Then tell us.

SIR GOOSE: Twas May 2nd in the year 1327 that (your Magasty came to the crown in the year 1310, 1st of March) Mr Hit stole your ring and in the same day soled it to Mr Icthus-oress but Icthus-oress did not know it was your ring, for Hit (old beast) had made it up to look like a comon ring.

[33]

KING BUNNY: I see, O but I don't see my ring and I'd like to.
SIR GOOSE: All right then. I know who can give it back.
    (*Enter* MR ICTHUS-ORESS *and* HIT.)
MR ICTHUS-ORESS: (*gives ring*) Theres the ring.
KING BUNNY: Gold Fish remove Hit.
    (*Exit* GOLD FISH. *Curtain.*)

Scene III: Cannon-Town. The docks. A wharf at the frith of the St
Bumble. A boat. (*On its back* SAILORS *round it and a* HARBOUR-MASTER.)

1st SAILOR: A hoy.
2nd SAILOR: Who speaks?
1st SAILOR: Me, Captain Tom's first boatswain.
2nd SAILOR: In sooth.
HARBOUR-MASTER: Get to work now. Paint this boat.
    (*exit*)
3rd SAILOR: (*aside*) O go and paint your nose.
    (*Exit all. Flourish. Enter* KING BUNNY, SIR PETER, MR MOUSE, GOLD
    FISH, SIR GOOSE, DORIMIE, MR ICTHUS-ORESS *and 2* SAILORS *guarding*
    HIT.)
KING BUNNY: Ah now we have got the old bar-man and whats beter still
    I have got my ring.
CHORUS OF VOICES: Hear hear.
KING BUNNY: O silence. And now I must say good by to Cannon-town,
    the town [of] my birth. Look hear Peter.
SIR PETER: Yes your Magasty.
KING BUNNY: Tell Sir Goose to tell Sir Big to tell Mr Gold Fish to tell
    Gollywog to tell Mr Icthus-oress to tell Dorimie to tell the sailors to take
    Hit away.
SIR PETER: Right sir.
    (*exit*)
KING BUNNY: Now I think we must go back to Mouse-land. Look the sun
    hath clove the earth in 2.[1]
    (*Curtain.*)

THE END

[1] The ancheint Mice believed that at sun-set the sun cut a hole in the earth for its self.

MANX AGAINST MANX

Sir Peter Mouse one night felt a nasty pain in the upper part of his tail, and on waking up began to wonder what it was. 'At last,' he said to himself, 'It was only a bad night-mare.'

However he found his tail mystereousely missing. 'This is odd,' said he. 'I must have had it cut off with-out noticing.' Next night he (in his sleep) witnessed a soreness at his nose. And in the morning what do you think? His whiskers were gone. 'Dear me!!' said Peter, 'This is bad.' The next night it snowed.

At 12 o'clock, in his sleep, Peter felt something hurting his ear. When he got up in the morning he found to his surprise that his left ear was cut off. 'Funny,' said Peter Mouse, and went out of the room.

Now Peter never spent money if he could help it, and as he was a detective he did not get another to do it for him. He went out into the snow and as he was walking down to his gate he saw paw prints. Mice often see that, but just behind the feet there was a little mark in the snow like this.

'A funny tail mark that is,' said Peter to himself. 'That mouse must have had his tail cut off like me. That is what I call a clue!' (I think you would too.)

Peter next went to Pip Castle for some clients were generly waiting for him. On his way home Sir Peter saw a large mouse with out a tail!! Peter did not go back to his house but followed the stranger for some distance, and then measured his foot-mark and made a picture of it.

Next night Sir Peter put a dummy of wood in his bed and he him-self sat up all night and watched from the garret window. Before doing so he set a 'non-killing' mouse-trap, it was like a small man-trap.

After watching for some time he saw a mouse coming twards the house. As soon as Mr No-Tail came near he got caught in the trap. 'Come and help me!' cried No-Tail as soon as he saw Peter at the window. Peter Mouse came out and let him go, then he asked No-Tail to stay the night with him. He took No-Tail in and gave him some beer then Peter led him up-stairs and gave him a bed, and as he slept went down to the polease office. Then he got No-Tail 'run in'.

THE RELIEF OF MURRY

We had been listening to Peter all the afternoon, but now we went out to enjoy the cool summer air. 'Peter' was the famous and illoustrius knighte Sir Peter Mouse and 'We' myself and some friends. Peter had been telling us a goode olde taile about a knight and his ladye. She was called Maude.

But we had got tired of the legande, the good knighte was telling, and perchance it was an easy one to get tired of. So we did come into the grounds of Pip Castle to enjoy ye fine summer winds.

Now quoth I to Sir Peter, 'Wilt go a-hawking on the banks of the Jemima my lord?'

'Sooth a goodly speech,' quoth Dorimie.

But Sir Peter said, 'Nay nay sirs more serios work is there than that. Hast not heard the news from Murry?'

'Nay tell it me good sir,' quoth I.

And Sir Peter said, 'The cats have beseiged Murry and it is like to fall into there hands if we do not send them help very soon.'

'Well gossip that is surely bad news,' said Dorimie, 'and if thy worship will consent we shall send help in the morning.'

'I my self will head the expedition. Huray!!'

Next morning after an early breakfast we started in the direction of Murry which we sighted in the late evening. It was surrounded completly by the enemyes tents. I realy felt quite thin as we skurried about among these rows

of guns and armed men (cats I mean). Once we were chalanged but we pretended to be a cat picket, then we camped in the shadow of a friendly forest.

In the early morning we covered our shining armour with dark cloaks and crept up behind the cat-sentrys back each and killed him. Then we rushed in and set fire to the hostile tents. The confusion was dreadfull. Everywhere the boom and sullen thunder of guns, the groans of the wounded the crackle of the fires and the wild shouts of 'Sir Peter for ever' then on 'In the name of the king!' When all of a suden the long fierce strain was over. The cats had fled. There camp was smoking ruins. Murry gates were open. The seige was raised!

HISTORY OF MOUSE-LAND
FROM STONE-AGE TO BUBLISH I
(OLD HISTORY)

(55 B.C.) Perhaps no greater country ever was seen in life than Mouse-land and yet one might have thought it might be ignorant oweing to its long 'stone-age' which lasted from B.C. 55 to – 1307!! How ever this was not the case. Mouse-land we find is the leading country of the globe!!

(51 B.C.) At first the Mouse-landers were divided into small tribes under chiefs, and continuly fighting with each other.

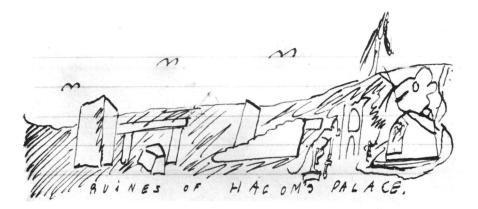

RUINES OF HACOM'S PALACE.

(49 B.C.) Hacom, chief of the Blue-Bottle tribe marched to Dorimie Castle and murdered the owner, namely Damus, for the sake of the castle and domain. (47 B.C.) He then took the castle, after which it was known as Hacom's Palace.

Damus in his life had been cheif of the Cosy Tribe, and his death did not disperse his tribe. When they heard of the murder they were very angry and determined to revenge thear king!! So they rose against Hacom and met at Hacom's Place in 43 B.C. where the castle was laid in ruins and Hacom slain. After which the Cosy became the most powerful tribe in the land.

[39]

A battle between Mice and Indians

In those days Mouse-land was called 'Bublish' and the mice called Bub-ills.

Shortly after the 'Melee of Hacom's Palace' (for so it shall be called) some inhabitints of Bombay came over to buy nuts. They taught the mice many things. The most important of which was: the use of money. Before that the Mice (or Bubils as they were called) exchanged things in markets. The Indians landed in 1216.

The Indians as it has been told gave knowledge to the Bublis. But the Bublies asked for some of it. The Bublis asked the Indians how they got on without fighting each others men. The asked ones told the Bubils that they choose a man to rule them all and called him Rajah or king.

The Bubils followed that plan. But no!! 'Out of the frying-pan into the fire.' Poor miss led creatures. Now they fought all the more!! Why? Because each mouse wished to be king. One had as much right to the throne as an other. So every place was fighting.

The new chief of the Cosy tribe was named after his country: 'Bublish'. He being the most powerful man[1] in the land raised an armie and marched to Dorimie Castle (the old one had been rebilt). When he got there he found that they had chosen another Mouse to be king named Poplar. Bublish pretendit to be quite loyal to him but *made him promise that after his death Bublish schould rule.*

BUBLISH I—FROM AN OLD MS

---

[1] Men live in Mouse-land.

INDIA = City with
900 people this = ◉
400 this = ◎ and so on ◦ ◦

Gulf-stream this ⟿

STATE OF TOUSAND-POT

NORMANTOWN

NORTHEAN-INDIA STRAITS

CONISTANTINOPLE
BOSPHORUS
TURKY
GLOBE

HIMILAYAS EVEREST

BEN GAL

DELHI
GANGES
N.E.R.
BANARES

DONIM-OO

WOLSCUSE

INDUS

CUTCH H.T.C.

DEVIL'S-BACK

CALCUTA

RUN OF CUTCH

CUTCH P.R.

CUTCH

CUTCH

MARATA

BOMBAY CENTRAL-INDIAN

ROWE

RAJAHSTOWN

DELHI-&-TIP-VIA-BOMBAY

HINDOOSTAN

S.N.R.

DUNKINSBY

GREAT CENTRA. RY.

JAMESTOWN

MADRAS

KALOON S.N.R.

PONDICHERRY

INDIAN OCEAN

CEYLON TUNNELL

ANTARCTICE

SOUTH SEA

COLUMBO

KANDY

CIRCLE

O-ROARA PRISON

HISTORY OF ANIMAL-LAND
(NEW HISTORY)

BOOK I

It is not my aim in writing this book to compile a full manual of Animal History but merely to set forth in consecutive order some more important facts.

CHAPTER I
INDIAN SETTLEMENT

The earliest written records of Animal-Land come from the Pongeeins. That nation, under its leader *Chin* conquered Animal-land when still a land of barbaric tribes. These records, however useful, are often impossible and many of them must be legends. Pongee seems to have held Animal-land until its downfall, when like all empires Pongee subsided. As soon as the Pongeein soldiers were withdrawn from Animal-land the numerous & bloody tribal struggles recomenced. The chief tribes were the Cosois, Draimes, Mansquoos & some others. The first notable event was the landing of some Indian settlers in the North of Animal-land. They landed near the Jemima River, in what was afterwards Mouse-Land. The Cosois, a tribe of Mice, whose chief was Hacom, received them well. The Indians stayed, intermarried with the mice, & helped against their hostile tribes.

About 100 yrs later the Indians advocated peace. The tribes agreed, & Hacom, grandson of the former Hacom, who had Indian ancestors on his mother's side, was elected King. He was the first proper King of 'Calico' as the northern part of Animal-land was then called. Long afterwards the southern states remained uncivilized. After this all the Indians returned to their own country.

Hacom used his power well. He called counsel of chiefs corresponding to our modern parliament. Without its consent nobody could be punished, or rewarded, nor could any new law be enacted. This assembled once a year.

[43]

Shortly after his 3rd Counsel Hacom crossed the borders of Calico with the idea of conquering Pig-Land. The pigs under their various chiefs (who had now united against Hacom, as a common enemy) advanced to meet him. The 2 armies met at a place called Kuckton (near where Marston now stands). Hacom fought well, and would have won had he not been outwitted by a clever feint on the part of the pigs. The Calician force was beaten, but still, much had been done towards the subjection of the pigs. Hacom was severly wounded by a stray arrow, but might have recovered, had he not been obliged to spend the night in the fields. It was winter, and the wound froze causing instant death. He had been an excellent king.

CHAPTER II
KING BUBLISH I

The people now chose Bublish, Hacom's 2nd cousin, to be their king. There was another heir nearer (Hacom's brother Johannus). But Bublish was very rich & powerful, and had many 'todies' and managed to get himself crowned instead. He christened the country 'Bublish' after himself, which was meant to be witty, but really only showed his conceit. He took it into his head that the soldiers (quartered in Pip-Castle) and their families were too friendly to Prince Johannus, and he was afraid lest they should rebel in his favour. So he held a fearful massacre of all inhabitants of Pip-Castle, men, women, and children. One person alone did he spare – Dormee, the governor of the Castle because he was sure of a good ransom for him. All through that year such brutal barbarities went on, so that it is often called 'Misery Year'. He refused to call the 'Damerfesk' as the counsel of Hacom was called; he set King Hacom's good laws (which he had sworn to keep & enforce) at defiance. However he carried his game too far even for himself. He had fancied his power shaken by the adherence of the Pip-Castle people to Johannus, but in reality it had been far more shaken by his own cruel massacre of them. His cruelty and deceitfulness roused all (except some of his own mercenaries) to revolt. And in the next year, a great rebellion headed by Johannus arose. The rebels broke their way into Murry Castle (partly owing to the treachery of Bublish's own mercenaries) and Johannus himself killed Bublish.

[44]

CHAPTER III
KING BENJAMIN

Johannus expected to be made king on the death of Bublish. But the counsel which he called pointed out in as complimentary a way as it could, that, though an excellent general, Johannus was quite unfit for the kingly office. Wisely he did not insist, and most generously giving way, allowed Benjamin (surnamed 'The Bunny') Duke of Rabbit-Land, to be peacably crowned in his stead. The new king begged Johannus not to retire into private life, and made him a 'Marshell', an entirely new title which was given to the chief General of the king's forces. Johannus complied with the king's wish, and remained an important person in the state. Benjamin was the grandson of Hacom, and therefore popular.

Johannus had not long been at his new post, as head of the Calician Army, before he had work to do; war broke out with Ojimywania, or Clarendon as it is now called. The cause of the war was this: in Bublish a certain Lord Giles, from Boot-Town (in the uncivilised south of Animal-land) emigrated to Ojimywania and became one of its great noblemen. He told Dracho, King of Ojimywania, many tales of Animal-Land and the Ojimywanians took advantage of the uncivilised condition of the southern states of Animal-Land to, in a kind of way, to appropriate them. At first they merely came and settled. Presently they took Boot-Town by storm, captured it, and drove out the inhabitants (who were mainly rats, and beetles). Johannus was busy putting down the cats, who had risen in rebellion, and did not hear of it. The first to notice the alarming power of the Ojimywanians in the south of Animal-land, was a young Gollywog with a very loyal heart, who made his way, with other Animal-landers from his home near Maine-Hoching, to Murry. On his way he encountered a band of 16 Ojimywanians, whom he put to flight. On his reaching Murry, he was made a Knight, and given a pension of 12 bresents[1] per year for life.

Benjamin now decided that the only thing to be done was to send Johannus and the army south. He did so and he himself went with the army. As soon as the Ojimywanians found out that the Calicians had heard of their inroads on the southern states, they made the most of their time, and seized

[1] Bresent – An Animal-Landish coin, amounting to 6/-.

[45]

as many towns and fortresses as they could. They even ventured as far north as Horse-Land, which was part of Calico. By the time Johannus and the king reached Horse-Land, they found that the enemies had gained possession of Maine-Hoching, the capital of that state. The inhabitants of the city met the Calician Army with tales of the injustice & cruelty they had suffered from the Ojimywanians, who, according to their custom, had driven out the citizens as soon as they gained the towns. So there were now no people in Maine-Hoching, but Ojimywanians. Johannus and the King laid seige to Maine-Hoching. For almost a year it bravely held out, but it was at length obliged to surrender. What remained of the garrison were treated with leniancy, but most of them had been killed during the seige, and many weaker ones had starved.

The army advanced, then, out of Calico farther south. Under the able leadership of Johannus and the King, nearly the whole of the south was cleared of Ojimywanians. Not content with this, the King organized a naval expedition to Ojimywania. He himself was to head it, & Johannus was to stay behind. Just before he went, the southern states begged that they might be united to Calico and all Animal-Land be one Kingdom. This was just what the Calicians wanted, and the union was effected.

Benjamin then sailed for Ojimywania leaving Lord Mearns, Mayor of Murry, as regent. The King and his division of the army gained no success in the expedition. After some fighting Benjamin was taken prisoner and would have been executed, had not Sir Jasper and his 2 sons bravely rescued him. Of the Jaspers we will hear more. Peace was made. As soon as the King was safely home, he made reforms in the 'Damerfesk'. In the days of Hacom it had been an assembly of *Chiefs*, so, later on it included the great nobles alone. So the common people had no say at all. King Benjamin with the help of his Chancellor Lord Big (a frog) passed many reforms giving 2 untitled commoners the right to come to the Damerfesk from each state.

Just now Johannus died of a fever. He was a great loss to the state, and his death was universally, and deservedly lamented.

About this time a mouse named Jas. Hit stole the Crown Jewels and escaping from prison, fled to Ojimywania. This effects Animal-Landish history because so many degenerate Animal-Landers fled to Ojimywania, and the ill-feeling between that country & Animal-Land increased until it seemed as if a second war was likely. Just at that point, the old King died. He was known as 'Benjamin the great'.

CHAPTER IV
THE ACCESSION OF KING MOUSE THE GOOD
AND THE FELINE REVOLT

He [Sir Peter Mouse] probably meant to go on to Englington, and, taking with him the soldiers quartered there, march to Cat-land and reduce the natives to submission. However, while his soldiers were encamped for the night, the Cats stole up with an enormous army–posted themselves on a hill, high above the mice; threw up a rampart of earth, placing there infantry (mostly bowmen) behind it, and their cavalry in front of it, ready to charge down the slope of the hill onto the mice (see map). While Sir Peter's army was still asleep, the cavalry charged down upon the camp, and did untold damage; then, before the mice could recover from their surprise or properlly arm themselves, the cavalry cleared away, and the bowmen shot their arrows into the camp. Then the whole Cat force swept down and the Mice were utterly routed. Sir Peter Mouse was slain and very few mice escaped. The Cats hotly pursued the few fugitives to Murry, and then beseiged the capital itself! The Cats sent home for more soldiers and more supplys. After almost a year and a $\frac{1}{2}$, (during which time the citizens suffered terrible privations), the seige was raised by 2 mice who had risen from the ranks; one of them was Thomas Jasper (son of Sir Jasper, who had rescued King Benjamin), and the other his friend Robert. How they did it is not certain, because so many stories about them are fables: but it is likely they did it by cunning: after this the Cats retired to their own state.

As soon as a good army had been collected Thomas and Robert went to Cat-Land. After a sharp short struggle, (the mice often fighting against tremendous odds), Cat-Land was conquered, and forced to unite with the rest of Animal-Land. The Cats attempt to conquer Mouse-Land did themselves a lot of harm: because, for many many years they were regarded with suspicion and hatred, and were not allowed to enjoy equal privilages with the other states of Animal-land.

All through this reign the crown had been very weak. So had the 'Damerfesk': in fact it had only been called twice in the whole reign! The great nobles, when not engaged in fighting the Cats, were usually carrying on private wars with their retainers. While the Southern States had become as uncivilised as they had been before the union. So, though in a Romantic

[47]

sense, Thomas and Robert had made it glorious, it was a bad reign, specially for the poor. Soon after the conquest of Cat-Land, the old king died, worn out by anxiety.

The end of the first Book

BOOK II
CHAPTER I

After the death of King Mouse the 'Damerfesk' was hastily called, to hold a consultation concerning who should next reign. The obvious hier to the throne was young Bublish: but the memory of his father's bad reign made him so unpopular, that he was exempted by a special act, and compeled to retire into private life. It was then decided that Animal-Land should be a Commonwealth or Republic. Lord Big (son of Sir Big, who had been executed by Sir Peter Mouse), tried to become 1st president (or 'governor', as he was then called) of the Commonwealth: but the nobles had had so much power in the last reign, and had so oppressed the poor, that the commons all over the country (under Balkyns, a Murry citizen,) revolted. Many nobles were murdered, and many castles destroyed. Balkyns approved of a Commonwealth, and made himself governer. The emancipation of the Commons would have been a good thing had they used their power, thus gained, well. But unhappily they used it exceedingly badly: they had no sympathy with persons who were not in the same rank of life, or did not fall in with their ideas.

Balkyns had an executioner called 'Thurlow'. This man was a marvelously good speaker. Now he used to be payed, not a fixed salary, but per execution: so whenever a person was being tried for his life, he (Thurlow), would come into the court and speak forcibly against the prisoner. By this, and other foul means, many perfectly innocent, honest people were put to death. It was nicknamed '2nd Misery Year', which recalled the brutal times of King Bublish. Just when things seemed likely to come to a crisis Balkyns died.

Sir Peter Mouse, son of Sir Peter of the last reign, marched down from Pip-Castle to Murry with a very large force. As all except a few of Balkyns' friends were heartily tired of his rule, Sir Peter Mouse met with little or no opposition; he called the 'Damerfesk'. Every-one agreed to continue the commonwealth, but to restore the power to the middle-classes. A Murry citizen named Perren, forcibly advocated a union between the parliaments of Animal-land and India. Through some extrodinary misunderstanding, this was regarded as treason. And Sir Peter and his friends, sentenced the good-hearted, but foolish Perren to be burnt. By the advice of Lord Twinkle-bury of Squirrel-Land, and some others, Sir Peter Mouse offered the governmentship of the commonwealth to Albert Leppi, a student of Eglington university. Leppi accepted it gladly, and was soon proclaimed governer.

CHAPTER II
GOVERNOR LEPPI I

The new governor proved to be the greatest scholar the Animal-Landers had ever seen, – but that was all. His talent for learning seems to have been more madness than anything else. He was cruel, foolish, stubborn, and weak. He first lent his confidence to Archbishop Quicksteppe who was well meaning, but narrow minded.

The most notable event which happened during the Quicksteppian Min-istry was the rise of the Chessaries. For a long time Chessmen had been hated and oppressed. They were scattered here & there, unhoused, hated, hunted & penniless. The first to try and improve their condition was a chess-king called Flaxman. He tried to build the first chessary near Boot-Town, in the reign of King Mouse I. He was mistrusted and misunderstood! So he emigrated to Tararo where the Chessmen prospered among the ami-able but primitive natives. During the Quicksteppian Ministry, he and his followers returned to Animal-Land, and this time gained more success. Two large Chessaries were founded, one at Boot-Town and the other at Murry; and also a smaller one at Peaktown. As the Chessaries were seats of learning (like universities): and as they lodged the poor at very low costs, they soon became popular with the peaple. Quicksteppe saw this and tried Flaxman for 'treason'. That noble Chessman was convicted and burned.

Sir Peter Mouse, then openly expressed his approval of the Chess move-ment: and in the next meeting of the 'Damerfesk' he attacked Quicksteppe, and was banished. Leppi, and his favourite had done a foolish thing for Sir Peter was popular. The Archbishop was murdered.

a small view of part of the Royal Chessary

THE CHESS MONOGRAPH
(PART I)

Chessaries, as we all know, are institutions for the lodging of Chessmen, for head-quarters of the Chess society, all over the world. When we look upon such a handsome edifice as the Royal Chessary (Murry), or the Northern Isle Chessary (Fuczy), we are inclined to take these things as a matter of course, and to think that Chessaries have been in existance, every since man lived in houses.

To correct this notion, we must carry our thoughts back to the 12th, 13th, 14th centuries: – and what shall we see there? We shall see Chessmen, few, scattered, unhoused, hunted, disliked, and pennyless, what a terrible state! Just as the Jews were treated in England at the same time; so were Chessmen treated, in Animal-land, India, Dolfin-land, Prussia, Pongee, and a great many more places, which I could mention, had I paper and time.

Not untill the early years of the 15th centuary, was any 'stir', so to speak, made at all. Then a certain Chess king appeared full of determination to put an end to the ill-treatment of his fellow-Chessmen. This individual, as no doubt you know, was the famous Gengleston Herbert Flaxman.

It is all very well to sit in your study reading this essay, and think of all the things in favour of Flaxman; but for him it was hard, very hard. Now: – a man in not *very* good circumstances wants to start an undertaking of great importance, and difficulties; – how can he begin? This was the problem which confronted King Flaxman, when first he got the idea. Never baffled, however, he tried to raise volantary contributions from Animal-landish people. This was worse than a failure, for it earned him the hatred of the people, who didn't trust in him. His idea was to found the first Chessary, near Boot; as we have seen, the difficulties in Animal-land had proved too insurmountable, so he must try elsewhere.

Accordingly (in company with 2 pawns, and a certain Castle Richards, who were faithful to him), Flaxman set-sail, in a trading ship, for Clarendon. On his arrival there the semi-civilised inhabitants made an attempt to (though they didn't mind the traders) drive out the 4 strangers. Flaxman, however, drove his way into the interior; and, having settled, sent a message back by the ship in which he came. This message was sent to Chessmen in India and Animal-land, telling them of Flaxman's scheme and bidding them come, – he would help with the expences. Soon they came: and the first Chessary in the world, of but 90 Chesspeople, was founded in Clarendon.

KING FLAXMAN

CASTLE
RICHARDS.

THO PAWNS

(FROM OLD PRINTS.)

In a former treatise I have describ-
-ed the foundation of thessaries,
and discussed the matter. In
that little work (owing to
lach of some requesites), I om.
-mited to say, (1.) How King
Flaxman put down the natives.
(2) How he paid for the build-
-ing of the thesary. (3.) Any-
-thing about thess orders, and
social organisation. On the
request of my father,
I am now penning an
essay to supply these
wants, or try to, rather.
In the first place we must
remember that Flaxman's
thersmen were civilised, and
had, naturalaly, better weap-
-ons than the crude and savage

(PART II)

In a former treatise I have described the foundation of Chessaries, and discussed the matter. In that little work (owing to lack of some requesites), I ommited to say, (1) How King Flaxman put down the natives, (2) How he paid for the building of the Chesary, (3) Anything about Chess orders, and social organisation. On the request of my father, I am now penning an essay to supply these wants, or try to, rather.

In the first place, we must remember that Flaxman's Chessmen were civilised, and had, naturally, better weapons than the crude and savage natives of Clarendon. But before the little colony of Chessmen could do anything, they must have somewhere to live in. Flaxman caused the Chess-people to work at the building of the Chessary, with their weapons on, as assaults were frequently made by the natives. The work, Flaxman decided, was to be done methodically: 2 or 4 men were always posted on the outskirts of the scene of labour, to warn the workers of an attack. One body of men felled the trees, another chopped them up, another carted them to the site of the Chessary, and a fourth body built. Flaxman did as much work as any other two put together!

In about a month the work was finished. And while they had been working, new Chessmen had been arriving, so they were now in a condition to fight.

ROUGH SKETCH OF THE BUILDING

ANIMAL·LAND.
RAILWAY
SKETCH·MAP.

RYS. = ⎯ MTS. ⬚

THE GEOGRAPHY OF
ANIMAL-LAND

Capital: Murry on the Jemima.

Animal-land is a dagger-shaped island lying West of the Great Continent. length 720 miles, breadth 380 miles, total area 110,600 sq. miles.

Surface: The mountains of Animal-land are numerous. The chief are: in the North the Mourme Mts. with point Phaze, and Mt. Donnair: in the South the Aya-Gutch Mts. with Mr. Podiphattea, and the Gorge di Diabolo 200 ft. deep: in the centre of Pig-land the Marston Hills, or the Marston Wolds. As well as many smaller ranges of hills, as the Dugg Hills in Horse-land.

Rivers: Animal-land is a very well watered country. The largest rivers are, the Jemima, the Poulder, the Maolar, the Great Hud, the Lack River, and the Little Hud on the East coast. The Bunyar, the Thoolnaar, and the Araboa: on the West coast. The Bushat on the North coast.

Animal-land is divided into 13 provinces.

Province	*Capital*
Bear-land	Figurdied
Wolf-land	Sclarustown
Squirrel-land	Fuczy
Mouse-land	Murry[1]
Rabbit-land	Cannon-town
Pig-land	Marston
Bird-land	Whing
Horse-land	Main Hocking
Fox-land	Sklyton
Land of Typical Animals	Brall
Insect-land	Boot-town
Rat-land	Tipp
With the island of Piscia, or Fishland	

[1] Mus-is = mouse.

[55]

Bear-land

Bear-land is situated in the north east of Animal-land. It is mountainous, and cold. In the south: the Ravine of Dirnom is the scene of the Animal-landish HIEMPIAL SPORTS.

Wolf-land

Wolf-land is scantly populated, and thinly covered with vegatation in the west where the soil is arid and sandy: timber however is largely grown in the north. Sclarustown its capital is of much importance, being a Great Northen Railway terminus.

Squirrel-land

Squirrel-land, owing to its magnificent mountains is much resorted to by tourests. Fuczy on Lake Fuczy is world-famed for *corn*. Great Eglington is an enormous railway centre.

Mouse-land

Mouse-land is the seat of government. Murry on the Jemima is a great port, and has imense shipbuilding yards. Here the Parliament is situated. It is a beautiful country of undulating hill and dale.

Rabbit-land

Rabbit-land is the first provence in learning and art. Cannon-town is so called because it is situated in the cannon of Butatsheek. Poultry are reared in the west.

Pig-land

Pig-land is very flat, and produces much coal and iron. Lake Marston is the largest expance of fresh water in the world. It is often called the Great Lake.

Bird-land

Bird-land is very uneven indeed. Whing is a university city, and is the terminus of the Bird-land Railway.

Horse-land

Horse-land is hilly and fertile. Large quantities of wheat, rye, rice, corn, and quicksilver. Main Hocking is the chief port for westward-going liners.

Fox-land

Fox-land is covered with forests, and tilled fields. Here ploughs were first made in 120 A.D. Potatoes are exported.

Viscount Puddiphat

BOXEN

*

BOXEN
or Scenes from Boxonian city life

THE LOCKED DOOR
AND THAN-KYU

THE SAILOR

"Mooring his boat, he stepped out"—

BOXEN

OR

Scenes from Boxonian
city life

I

Night was falling on the Bosphorus as the town guardsman sighted a small but tidy schooner tacking up to Fortressa. For'rad stood a young Tracity Chessary Pawn & at the tiller a sturdy thickset knight stolidly smoking his pipe. With a little deft maneouvering he brought her up a secluded rocky creek & dropt anchor about 200 yds. from the shingle. He called the assistance of the Pawn to lower his solitary boat, which soon was lying under the schooner's counter, & several vigorous strokes sent him to the beach. Mooring the boat he stepped out & in the dusk descried two tall athletic figures walking along a short distance away.

'Why! Your Majesties!'[1]

They turned.

'Macgoullah.'

'At your service. What are you doing here?'

'Oh,' said the 'Jah, 'Learning Turkish.'

'Alone?' inquired the knight.

'No. Big's here,' answered Bunny.

'At the inn?'

'Yes.'

The three friends walked together to the postern gate, where the guard admitted them for a small fee. A few hundred yds. brought them to the inn. Through the door into the Inner room Macgoullah caught sight of a stout frog in evening dress.

'I'll stay in the Outer,' he observed.

---

[1] The kingdoms of Boxen although united in Parliament retain their monarchs, the Rajah of India & the King of Animaland.

Macoullagh decides to stay in the Outer.

The boys walked into the Inner. It was a small room crowded to over-flowing. Round the table sat Puddiphat, Goose, Quicksteppe, & the Little Master.[1]

'Boys where have you been?' asked the Frog.

'Oh nowhere special,' returned the 'Jah with characteristic vagueness. Big gulped & continued bisecting a portion of cod. All present were Boxonians except one Prussian who sat in a far corner silent & morose, unoticed by all: true their was a cautious look in Quicksteppe's grey eyes, but no one observed it. The company bent over their meal & conversation & quietly the Prussian slipt into a curtained cupboard. Big looked up.

[1] 'Little Master', was the speaker of the Parliament, and had many powers, including that of being the constant guardian & adviser of the kings. The present one, Lord Big, exercised much influence over King Benjamin & the Rajah, as he had been their tutor in their youth: in private he neglected all the usual formulae of adress to a prince: To wit next line 'Boys . . . etc'.

'Are we alone?'

'Yes, my dear Little Master,' said Goose.

'Now Goose: tell your tale.'

'Yes. Gentlemen I have just found that the whole Clique is threatened by Orring one of the members for "the aquarium" – '

'Come, my good bird,' cried Big, 'what does that mean?'

'For Piscia, my good Frog,' – Big gulped – 'has determined to throw all the present clique out of office: & is bribing right & left.'

'It is impossible,' cried the Frog, 'the M.P.'s are incorruptable.'

Quicksteppe inquired 'How, Goose, do you know this?'

'Because friend Green – '[1]

'That parrot?' gasped Big.

'Yes Little Master. Because he overheard at the Murryman's rest – '

'That place?' gasped the worried Frog.

Yes. He overheard Orring.'

Big rose. 'Come boys. Its late,' he said.

Quicksteppe, he, the boys, & Chutney went out. They passed through the Postern gate, & strolled along the shingle: Their house was in the outer town.

Presently Big removed his cigar and said, 'Polonius Green overheard it? What would he wish to tell it to Goose for? He is no friend of mine.'

'Its rather deep,' said Quicksteppe.

'Ah yes,' said Bunny.

'There's some dirty work going on,' asserted the Little Master.

A few more steps brought them to their house, & to bed. Long after the others had gone to sleep Quicksteppe lay thinking. What interest had that Parrot in the crisis? It might prove of the utmost importance. But how should he find out? Who, whom he could trust, moved in Green's circles? He put the question to himself & next moment had the answer. Macgoullah!! Of course. The shrewd, honest master of the schooner Bosphorus was his man. True the Bosphorus was engaged in somewhat shady business but no one could deny that its captain was honest & patriotic. Of course he never thought for a moment that Green had told Goose through a disinterested motive. But having decided on a plan of campaign he turned over & slept.

[1] Polonius Green, a parrot of low birth, & the owner of a line of colliers.

[63]

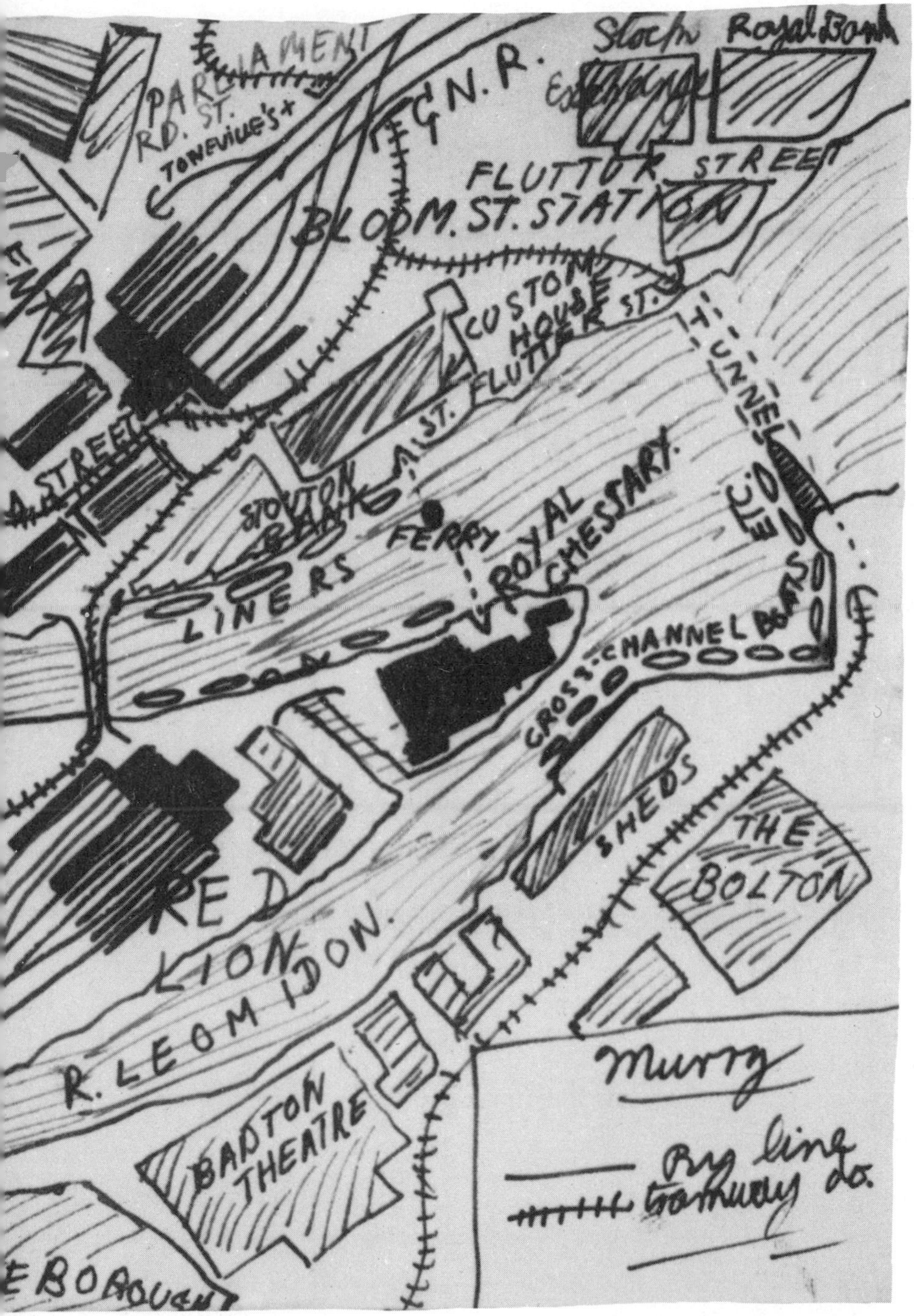

'The boys,' the two sovereigns of Boxen, had come to Fortressa under the charge of the Little-Master to rub up their Turkish. But this onerous duty did not prevent some enjoyment. Turkey was ever dear to the boys: it was such a change. Turkey where all sorts of things like slavery, brigands, & bazaars still existed. On the morning after the night described above, the two kings rose early, dressed in flannels & taking towels stole out of the hired house, & down to the beach.

'A ripping day 'Jay,' observed Benjamen.

'Glorious. Hullo their's a boat, new since last night,' cried his companion eagerly, indicating a big untidy Turkish tramp.

'Can you read her name?' asked the Rabbit.

After a moment the Rajah spelt out 'The Demetrie. I suppose she [is] a Hamman Liner.'

They now turned their attention to their matutinal bathe. This office performed they dressed & strolled back. Presently they encountered another. He was a short well-knit owl, gordiously attired in a morning-coat & white tall hat. He was smoking a huge cigar.

'My dear Puddiphat.'

'Good morning, Majesties.'

'Up early for once, Puddles?'

'As usual,' retorted the Owl, & walked on with an elaboroute bow.

'I'm very fond of him,' remarked the Indian as soon as they were out of hearing.

'So am I. Why does Big object to him?'

'Oh he doesn't really.'

'Well I think its because of his owning those music-halls.'

'The Alhambras!'

'Yes. Of course Big does'nt like that.'

They strolled into the house & found the others preparing to go to the inn for breakfast.

'Boys,' said the Frog indicating the kings' flannels, 'you're not going in those things?'

'Yes,' said Bunny in a hurt voice.

Big sighed: & they started for the inn. All except Quicksteppe who said he was unwell. As soon as they were gone he hastened into a hat, & started down the beach, at a really remarkable rate for so old a gentleman. The Bosphorus was sailing this morning with Macgoullah on board! And he must get Macgoullah!

Alas, his toilet had taken too long. When he reached the jetty the Bosphorus was a good mile out! A lean swift row-boat for hire, manned by three Chessmen came along side. The leader spoke: –

'Does your Excellency wish a boat?'

Quicksteppe clutched at the straw.

'Yes,' he cried jumping in, '5 sovereigns if you catch up that schooner!'

'Yes Excellency.'

In an incredibly short space of time the lean craft was shooting through the water with the general in the stern sheets. But it soon became painfully obvious that the persuers were loosing ground. A fine fresh breeze had caught the vessels sails & under her sturdy master's fine manipulation was fast dissapearing over the sky line.

I I I

Any sailor who has been to Murry knows the Murryman's rest. This servicable inn stands on the Royal Wharf & is a spacious building whose architecture presents a hetrogenious appearance as fresh wings have been built on from time to time through the 2 last centuries. On a certain morning about three days after Quicksteppes abortive attempt to catch the Bosphorus, Polonius Green sat in its cosy Inner.[1] He was seated on a high-backed oaken bench, beside a Foreigner. The latter was a clean shaven man with flowing red hair.

'Well,' the captain was saying, 'what is the do?'

'The "do" is,' said the other coldly, 'that you have made a fool of yourself.'

The bird bristled.

'What do you mean, Sir?'

'Just this. You have told Goose that our leader was bribing.'

'Yes. But –'

'Well? – '

[1] Boxonian inns have usually 2 rooms, the Inner or 1st class, & the Outer or 2nd.

'Our Leader declared that he would not give me a place in the new Clique. So I naturally – '

'Yes. Because you can set no bounds to your insatiable ambition you overthrow the whole party?'

'I do!' said the angry bird.

'Animal-lander! Sparrow!'

'Prussian!'

'How was it you fell out with our leader?'

'Mind your own business.' With that, the bird, with ruffled feathers, paid his bill & went out. The Prussian gazed after him with angry eyes, & sank back on his bench.

'D—n the bird!!' he muttered. At that moment the doors of the Inner were thrown open & another customer entered. He was a short, fairly stout bear. His fur was of a rich hock-brown color, & well oiled on the top of his round head. His expression was humurous, self satisfied, & intelligent. A cigarette was grasped between his tightly pursed lips. He was clad in a steward's uniform and his cap bore the legend, 'H.M.S. THRUSH'. The Prussian looked up.

' 'morning Mr Bar.'

'Delighted to see you my dear Glohenman.'

'Where have you sprung from?'

'Oh the Thrush is at the Lord Wharf.'

'Never! And captain Murry on board?'

'Oh yes.'

'And Hogge, the mate?'

'1st officer,' corrected R.N. [Bar, of the Royal Navy], 'but how is business?' The foreigner looked round. They were alone.

'Clique business?'

'Yes.'

Then the two drew close together & for a long time sat in close confabulation. The Bear seemed to give instructions, & the other now & then made notes in a large pocket book. Occasionally he offerred suggestions: suddenly, after about a quarter of an hour, to one of these suggestions the steward rose, & said loudly 'No we will never do that. And don't get beyond yourself either, my friend.' Then he went out banging the door.

Left alone the Prussian took another glass & reflected that these cursed Boxonians were all fools.

"--another customer entered--"

The pig in his office

IV

The manager's room of the offices of Pig & Bradley Shipowner & Carriers Ltd in D Street Murry, betrayed by its appurtenances the tastes & character of its owner. One wall was almost entirely filled up by three huge windows which brilliantly illumined the apartment. The floor was covered by a well worn oilcloth of the conventional light brown. To the right & left stood huge glass-fronted bookcases filled with all volumes necessary to a shipowner, arranged according to authors. On the fuorth wall hung a large map. In the middle of the room was a large double table for the partners. Only Mr Reginald Vant (the Pig) was at this time present. He was a pig of some 40 summers, shrewd, hard working & unaffected. His face at present betrayed no emotion but interest in the papers before him. He was clad in one of those respectibally plain stuff suits so dear to the business-man. Suddenly he was enterrupted by a clerk who said that Mr Green wished to see him, if he was not busy.

'Admit him,' said the Pig, pushing aside his work.

A minute later the parrot entered, looking annoyed for he had come straight from the Murryman's Rest. The Shipowner bade Green sit & gave him a pipe of Montserrat[1] which the latter sucked while they talked.

'My dear Mr Green, what can I do for you?'

'Only give me a little information Sir.'

'At your disposal. Biscuits? – '

'Please. How's trade?'

'Just as usual. But what is the information you want?'

'This. I hear that a certain Mr Glohenman is applying for one of your captaincy's.'

'That's so.'

'Is he Mr Philip Glohenman, or the brother?'

'The brother, Mr Green.'

'Ah. They are much devoted to each other.'

'So I blieve.'

Pig paused. Then said, 'Do you know the two Glohenmans?'

'Exceedingly well, Mr Pig.'

'Well you as a seaman can advise me. Is this man a good captain?'

'Really Sir, I cannot stop to give you a character now, but I will come to morrow.'

'Very well.'

The two shipowners shook hands & the bird went out. 'What,' thought Pig, 'was his game?'

V

Mr Green was highly satisfied with his morning's work. He now was even with Glohenman. He knew perfectly well that Capt. G. was a Prussian agent & that it was all important that he should get a place in the Pig Line. Prussia wanted an insight into Boxonian commerce & were depending on this man to give it them. He knew also that Captain Glohenman's chance of getting the position depended on the character which he – Polonius – gave him before Pig. He had now only to confront the captain's devoted &

---

[1] 'Pipe of Monsterrat' – a glass of Montserrat wine sucked through a straw or pipe.

patriotic brother with these facts, & he had him at his beck & call. Philip Glohenman would have his brother in the Pig line at all costs. And now that he had this devoted Philip, how should he use his power? The answer was 'to get myself into the Clique'. Orring, the leader of his party, had refused to get him a place. But Philip had unbounded influence over Orring, so the worthy bird was full of confidence.

On the same morning, at 6 o'clock the steamer Ariadne (C.I.Ry) had arrived from Bombay having on board Lord Big, their Majesties, Visc. Puddiphat & General Quicksteppe. Although she arrived at Player's Wharf so early, their Majesties and the viscount were up an hour before she was in. The Owl was as immaculate as ever, in a brown lounge suit & a Homburg hat of the same color. The two kings were in grey tweed & high spirits, busily engaged in explaining everything to each other – a superfluous occupation as there was nothing which one knew & the other did not. The viscount gave their Majesties to understand that he was interested in all they told him. The Little Master presently joined the party.

'Boys, have you not got coats on?'

'No,' replied the 'jah.

'Are'nt you cold?'

'No,' replied the rabbit.

Arrived at Player's Wharf, the viscount took his leave of the royal party & jumping into a hackney cab ordered it to drive to the Goose[1] for breakfast. Puddiphat's thoughts were of the sweetest as he lent back on the richly upholstered seat & watched the panorama of Murry streets flitting past. Turkey bored the Owl: he loved Boxen & Murry above all the cities of Boxen. His numerous Alhambras[2] were paying excellently. This pleasing reverie was broken in upon by the vehicle drawing up outside the Goose Inn. The young Owl grasped his cane & stepped out, & entering the Inner Coffee Room sat down. He had hardly begun his breakfast when a female music-hall 'star' walked up to speak to him. She was chiefly remarkable for an impossible hat & an irritating laugh. Towards Puddiphat she adopted the condescending air which actresses always do towards managers. The subject which they discussed was apparently of some interest, & after some con-fabulation the Owl got up & going out said,

[1] The Goose Inn, the 1st Murry restaurant and hotel.
[2] He was the owner of several Music-halls over the country, called the Alhambras.

'Yes, a splendid idea.'

The result was that a couple of days later The boys, Pig, Colonel Chutney, Fortescue, Mr Hedges[1] (The Beetle), also Walking Waggon – Boxen's best comedian, Rosie Leroy the inimitable comedienne, & Phyllis Legrange comedienne & dancer (the promoter of the scheme), each recieved the following message: –

Visc. Puddliphat, requests the pleasure of
‗ ‗ ‗ ‗ ‗ ‗ ‗ ‗ ‗ ‗ ‗ ‗ ‗ 's
company at supper
8.30,   Sat. April 3rd /12.
R.S.V.P

VI

A day after The Owl sent out his invitations, a neat little schooner came along side the Royal Wharf: she was none other than our old friend the Bosphorus under command of sturdy Macgoullah. And very glad he was too to be once more walking up to the Murryman's Rest. When he had got comfortably settled in the homely Inner with a pipe & a bottle of Vin-de-Brus (for he was rich though plain) he was disgusted by an interruption. The door was flung open & a tall, liveried valet entered.

'Sir,' he said, 'do I address Captain Macgoullah?'

'Yes.'

'My master, General Quicksteppe, desires your presence please, if you can come Sir?'

The honest chessman, who had looked forward to a morning at his favorite Inn, was somewhat annoyed, however he felt it incumbent upon him to follow the valet to a motor waiting on the Royal Wharf. Shortly after he had gone Green & Herr Glohenman stalked into the Inner & sat down.

---

[1] Manager of the R.S.Ry., a shrewd business man but a gay enough person in his moments of leisure.

[73]

'Glohenman, I brought you here for an important purpose.'

'What?'

'I must have a place in the new Clique.'

'Well? I can't help you – '

'You must.'

'How so?'

'Listen! Your brother is trying to get a place in the Pig line.'

'How do you know that?'

'Never mind. I *do* know. Now Pig has asked me for his character. Pig trusts me.'

'But, you – '

'You have influence with Orring. It is a case of either-or.'

Meanwhile Macgoullah had been shown into a salon in the General's townhouse, where he stood feeling very uncomfortable & awaiting the owner. Presently a door was opened & the old man entered.

'Good morning, my dear captain.'

'Good morning, m'lord. What can I do for you?'

'Well captain, of course what I am going to say won't go beyond you?'

'No, m'lord,' replied Macgoullah, begginning to feel uncomfortable.

'Have you heard anything about this movement against the Clique?

'Er – yes m'lord.'

'Well, you are a Walterian?'[1]

'I think so M'Lord.'

'Well you know Captain Green?'

'Yes m'Lord.'

'Well could you assist me in watching him?'

'I could not, m'lord,' cried Macgoullah who was thoroughly sick of the business. 'You'll have to get up very early to get the better of Green.'

'Then, you won't help me?'

'I'm afraid I can't,' replied the sailor, honestly disstressed at the other's dissapointment.

[1] Walterians & Diripians were the 2 rival Parties. W's upheld old ideas & D's wanted reform & a new Clique as the old had held office very long.

In the cloakroom at Puddiphat's.

VII

On the evening of the eventful Saturday, their Majesties were turning Riverside Palace upside down in their preparations for The Owl's select supper party. They forgot it till they had only quarter of an hour to dress: however after almost superhuman efforts they got into their car in time. After a short drive they stopped outsides Puddiphat's magnificent town-house. Stepping out, they were shown into a cloak room crowded with guests, talking in subdued tones & brushing hair & trowsers. For some time they stood politely pushing each other to the door. At last Pig made a bold sally & walked with a large following to the reception-room.

'My dear Puddiphat!'

'Delighted Mr Vant. Evening Waggon: you know Reggie the cod – no? Mr Vant – Mr Waggon.'

The bird was resplendent in his evening dress & piqué shirt. He moved off.

'Why your Majesties. I am much honored.'

Presently Phyllis Legrange walked up.

'Good evening Miss Legrange. You have never met their Majesties? His Majesty King Benjamen – Miss Legrange etc. Take the rest said.'

'Good evening,' said Bunny nervously, 'Er – have you been to Sangaletto?'[1]

'No,' replied Miss Legrange, 'I never go to operas.'

'I hate them,' said the rabbit, feeling it was what he should say.

'Oh Your Majesty! That's very bad taste.'

Then they both laughed politely.

Meanwhile the host was busy elsewhere. 'My dear Beetle!' he said to Hedges, 'How are the railways? Hullo Chutney. Good evening Miss Leroy. Colonel Chutney – Miss Leroy. Miss Leroy – Colonel Chutney. Why there's Fortescue. How's trade? Have you heard Sangaletto? No? – Oh you should.'

'Who's singing Sangaletto himself?' inquired the 'jah who had come up.

'Vön Oscar Wûlles. He's awfully good your Majesty. I suppose you're going?'

' 'Fraid so,' said the monarch.

'Why,' broke out the Owl, 'Don't you know Miss Leroy?'

'Oh yes,' said the Rajah, 'I had the pleasure of being introduced at Chutney's ball last season.'

'Friends,' announced the host, 'Supper is ready.'

'May I have the pleasure?' said the 'jah to Rosée Leroy, while Bunny applied the same question to the amiable Phyllis. The whole party adjourney to the supper room where the table groaned under cold ham & chicken, salads, oysters, wines & other delecacies. Everyone got freeer & more interesting. Walking Waggon told his best stories, Puddiphat made doubtful jokes & the rest talked, listened & laughed. The 'jah related stories about the Little Master, who was heartily laughed at & afterwards toasted. Then followed toast upon toast, their Majesties of course leading the list. Then as the last stroke of 12 ceased to vibrate, the Owl said, 'Let us take the air.'

With that they issued forth, hatless & bootless to roam the city.

---

[1] A grand opera of the heaviest type.

VIII

On the night of the eventful Saturday the Little Master had been to a select political debate at Sir Goose's chambers & was returning in his brougham at 2 in the morning. Leaning back upon the luxurious cushions he had almost fallen asleep when the strains of a music hall song sung by many voices startled him,

> 'Oh Mister Puddiphat
> Where did you get that ha–at?'

Such a staid & sober individual as the Frog was annoyed at the idea of any party going out after supper in this manner. Without reflecting who the bounders were he dozed off again. Suddenly –

> 'Now down D. street we will go
> That's the place for us you know
> Whoop!!'

just besides the coach, which had abruptly stopped. Next instant, to his untold horror, the door was flung open & a crowd of people stood outside.

'Morning, Sir' cried one merrily. It was the Owl!

'Puddiphat!' cried Big in horror. 'And (he gasped) your – your – majesties!' It was only too true. There, before the little-master's gaping eyes stood the sovereigns of Boxen, bare-headed, & worse, singing a music-hall song at 2 in the morning, & worse & worse each with a music hall actress!! Behind them surged Pig, Beetle & the others.

'Your Majesties,' said he icily, 'come in & come with me to the palace!'

'Not at all Big' protested the 'jah. 'You come out.'

'Your Majesties! By a little-master's authority I request you to come. Upon my word if you don't I'll resign!'

'But what's the matter?' asked Bunny.

Soon however the kings sulkily got in, the doors were shut, & the carriage swept on. As soon as they were settled Big said, 'Boys. This is awful.' 'But my dear Big –'

'Benjamin!!' this sternly. The rabbit collapsed onto the seat.

Then Big muttered in a dull fatalistic way he had when annoyed, 'You ought to be deposed.'

'Wish we could,' laughed the 'jah.

Seeing that he could make no impression on them the Frog was silent while the carriage rapidly drove to Riverside where at last all three thoroughly annoyed staggered to bed.

IX

His Majesties gunboat Thrush to which Mr Bar belonged in the capacity of Purser & Master of the commisariat was a tidy vessel of some 500 odd tons. Five of her crew birthed aft, namely Murray, the skipper, Hogge the 1st officer, Williamson, the gunnery officer, Macfail, the 1st engineer, & last but not least Bar the purser. Just at present she was a day out from Murry on her voyage to Floe, & it was the captain's watch. Suddenly the look-out reported the Pig-liner Dolfinian on the port bow. Quarter of an hour later the two boats were within haling distance of one another, & Captain Murray ordered the other to stop. In a short time the gig was lowered & the inspection was made. Among other casual facts which the captain happenned to notice was that the 1st mate was a Prussian. Bar only among the Thrush's crew realised that it was Glohenman's brother & how he had got there.

A day later after the Dolfinian had got in Green & Philip Glohenman sat in the Inner of the Murryman's rest.

'Well my friend,' said the parrot, 'Your brother, as you see, is safely in the Pig line.'

'Yes, my dear bird. I can never express my gratitude.'

Polonius looked sharply up.

'Eh! What about my cliqueship?'

'Mr Green?'

'I thought we had a bargain.'

'No, no, Mr Green.'

The parrot was furious.

'You promised me a cliqueship,' he repeated doggedly.

'My good bird, this parrotlike repetition is most annoying.'

Leaving the speechless bird, the Prussian rose & strode out. The unfortunate Green was unable to compell him to carry out their compact. He of course could not bring it before a court or he would be putting his own head in the noose for blackmail. Suddenly he remembered that he had arranged to go with Macgoullah that evening to Sengeletto.

[78]

Polonius gets left.

X

On the Friday after the ever memorable Saturday the Murry Opera House was crowded with people attracted to Sengelleto by the vocal powers of Wullês, Mlle. Armanche, & the rest of the fine company. There in the dress circle are Pig & Bradley, in the stalls Hedges & others of his type. There too was Goose in his box, Puddiphat with Pyllis Legrange, both looking immensely bored. There were Quicksteppe & Chutney who share a box. All eyes were directed upon the royal box, which as yet was empty. In the pit sat Green & Macgoullah, the later fortified with a gladstone bag of oranges. Presently the door of the Royal box opened & in walked the two kings followed by the Little Master walked in.

[79]

'A good house Big,' said the 'jah.

'Boys!' said the Frog suddenly.

'Yes.'

'Look at that Owl,' said Big, despairingly indicating the opposite box which contained Puddiphat, & 'who's that woman?'

Meanwhile in the owl's box another animated conversation was going on.

'I say Puddles,' said Phyllis, 'Who's that toad in the Royal Box?'

'It's a good job he didn't hear you call him a toad. He's the Little Master.'

During the dialogue the orchestra had begun to attack the overture with great vigour & spirit, but she continued in a loud tone.

'Listen to that Puddles. Do you call that music?'

'It is usually thought so.'

'Hush' came from various parts of the house, especially the pit. Phyllis leaned out of the box & blissfully unconscious that she was referred to said, 'What on earth are the people in the pit making that noise for?'

'I believe they're annoyed at out talking,' rejoined Puddiphat in a hurt tone. 'Hullo, we're getting to business.' And indeed the curtain was rising on the first scene of the great opera. Big settled down to sleep, Puddiphat retired to the bar, & Macgoullah set in on his oranges. Goose annoyed everyone near him by humming out of tune: the boys settled down to a conversation which lasted till the drop scene fell on the impassioned strains of Marita's great aria. The boys strolled out & across to Puddiphat's box.

'Good evening, Majesties.'

'Puddiphat. Good evening Miss Legrange,' said the rabbit.

'What do you think of it Puddles?' inquired the rajah.

'Oh very good, excellent,' said the Owl, 'What I heard of it.'

'Yes,' said Phyllis, 'he's been out all the time.'

'And what,' said the 'jah turning to her, 'did you think?'

'To be frank, Your Majesties, I thought it great rubbish.'

Just at this point the prelude to the 2nd act began & the boys returned to their own box. The second act was famous only for a chorus of prisoners which caused Puddiphat & his fair companion to yawn more than before. As the curtain fell, the manager sent an attendant to tell Goose that he must stop humming or else go out. Meanwhile the pit was talking also.

'Well?' said Polonius.

'Ah it's cod,' said Macgoullah.

'Cod!?' cried the musical Green aghast, 'I'd like to see you write it!'

"—till the dropscene fell"

'I wouldn't!' said Macgoullah, 'Try another orange?'

The curtain now rose upon the 3rd act. Meanwhile in the bar a different conversation was going on. It was occupied by two Prussians, Philip Glohenman & another.

'The bird actually blackmailed me. And now he wants me to get him a cliqueship.'

'Well,' said the stranger, 'get him one. Our object is to place the new Clique under an obligation to us.'

'But my dear Dangle, do you think that I would trust to their mere gratitude?'

'I suppose not, but you must conciliate him. In Turkey at Fortressa I overheard a conversation in an inn & it seems he's been telling things to Goose.'

'I might make a bargain –'

'Yes.'

The dropscene fell some hours later on the 8th & last act of the opera & as the audience walked out no one thought less of the piece than Philip Glohenman. But he thought.

XI

H.M.S. Thrush had a great liking for the port of Marston on the Great Lake. Thither she wended her way immediately on her return from Floe. And so one evening Bar might have been seen talking to the manager of The Lake Inn.

'Yes, Mr Bar?'

'Can you tell me is there a Mr Orring staying here?'

'Yes Mr Bar. Do you wish to see him?'

'Yes.'

Bar followed the manager to a private sitting room. Here he found Mr Orring, an elderly lizard. The manager left them.

'My dear Bar.'

''Evening. I come on business.'

'You come on business?'

'Yes. About your new Clique.' He spoke curtly.

'Ah!'

'It appears you've quarrelled with Green.'

'Yes: he's a most provoking bird.'

'Well, you've got left!'

'How!?'

'Green and your Prussian friends & the others have undertaken to oppose tooth and nail any bill *you* bring in. Also they're going to draw up a new bill leaving you out! A very good thing too. But d—n it all they've forgotten me as well!!'

The little bear was furious. He ruffled his well oiled fur, he flung things about the room. The lizard was despairingly calm. Presently he said, 'Its all up Mr Bar. Its a hopeless job. My work has been useless.'

'I told you that these Prussians would be the ruin of it!!'

'Well this is no time for regrets. I will this evening start for Piscia, & live privately. I shall be practically ruined. I promised all in the League Clique-ships. I promised £400 compensation each if the plan failed.'

—"The little bear was furious"—

[83]

Bar was so genuinely distressed at the other's fix that he forgot his own dissapointment.

'Oh no Mr Orring. I for one would never touch a penny of it, & I am sure none of the others would. It was only ill luck. On the contrary we will all respect you for your effort & sympathise with your misfortune!'

'It was not luck. It was my foolishness in quarelling with that bird. Of course I shall pay. It was my fault. Good evening.'

Bar went out more annoyed than he could say. But he saw the other would be better alone to think out a plan.

XII

The unhappy lizard's position was indeed most unenviable. He was not originally rich when he had brought in the motion for the new clique, but he was a somewhat unscrupulous reptile and spent money like water in bribing here & there: doubtless he hoped to refind it when he became the new Little Master. Let it also be said for him that he thought the means justified his end. Then half way through, the foreigners threatened to back out & inform if they were [not] silenced with another fabulous bribe. And so when the blow fell Orring had had just enough to keep things going till the motion was carried. Now to 5 people he owed £400 (the 5 who had been promised Cliqueships) & to the other members of the League, of whom there were about 10 he owed 300 each. The Prussians now demanded a silence fee of £700 each, which he must pay or go to jail for bribery. The debts were –

5 Cliqueships	£2000.
League	£3000.
3 Prussians	£2100.
Total	£7100.

That night he sat up late in his room, thinking, when suddenly a knock at the door broke in upon his reverie.

'Come in.'

'Mr Orring?'

'Yes Sir.'

'This letter for you.'

'Thanks.'

The man went. And on opening the letter the lizard's joy knew no bounds. It was a document to state that 'Arnold Olderwell, gentleman, deceased, does give & bequeath to his cousen James Orring £100,000.'

XIII

The city of Murry read by a notice in every inn that on Monday, Parliament would assemble. Among the first to read the notice was General Quicksteppe as he sat down to breakfast in the Inner of the Goose. So the blow had fallen! Although the official notice did not state the business which was to be discussed, the old strategian knew. These beggars had brought in their new Clique bill. The present Clique of which he was a member had been in office for over two years & it was only natural that it should fall to peices sooner or later. His attempt to make an ally of Macgoullah had failed: the captain was too busy in his own work to take up politics. Presently Colonel Chutney sat down at the same table.

'Good morning, General.'

'Why, that's you Chutney. Were you at the opera?'

'Yes. Do you see about the session?'

'Yes. I suppose that means a new Clique.'

'Yes. We won't be in it if there is?'

'No. Hullo here's Puddiphat. My good owl –'

' 'Morning. Do you see the notice –?'

'Yes. A new Clique   '

'No,' said the viscount. 'Because, look here. Orring the leader of the movement has gone home to Piscia & settled down.'

'Rubbish!'

'It is true.'

'Then there isn't going to be a new Clique?'

'Oh no. We are quite safe.'

Meanwhile in the Inner of the Murryman's rest the situation was also being discussed by Green and Glohenman.

'Do you hear,' cried the parrot, 'that that lizard has given it up!'

'Well, we weren't going to have him in it any way.'

'No, but I wonder who told him?'

[85]

" Rivals in the rostrum.

XIV

On Monday very few members failed to attend the debate. The Murry House, a spacious building situated on Watermans Road, was crowded to its full. There on an obscure back bench sat Mr Green, interested & excited: there is Mr Bar with Captain Murray winking at their friends in the gallery. There also in the gallery sit the two Glohenmans: there on the front bench is Macgoullah in a new blue serge suit & a clean wooden pipe, looking very bored. The Clique (whose days even now are numbered), consisting of Quicksteppe, Colonel Chutney, Goose, Puddiphat, & Pig, & presided over by their Majesties & the Little Master are absent in the Clique-room. But all eyes are fixed on the door by which they come in. Presently it opened & the Clique, loudly cheered, filed in, M'Lord Little Master & the Kings seating themselves on the raised triple throne. Big rose & walked to the rostrum: 'Your Majesties, & gentlemen of the house: we are met here to day to discuss Mr Orring's new Clique Bill. This honourable member however has not turned u– is not present. Consequently, unless any of his party wish to bring in a new Clique Bill we will – '

'I do M'Lord,' this from the parrot.

'Very well. Will you please speak on it?'

'I should imagine so,' said Green brusquely.

Big tiptoed back to the throne & whispered to the Rajah 'That parrot!'

The latter meanwhile began to speak: – 'Your Majesties, Little-Master & gentlemen of the house: in bringing in this bill, I'm not going to have any pother like some learned friends' – (Big outraged) – 'I'll be plain: It strikes me, that this Clique has had its fair share.' (laughter: 'Order!' from the usher) 'India is not equally represented with Animalland.' (At this juncture Puddiphat & Pig got out & went to be bar.) 'I propose fer the new Clique – ' (Big whispered 'Ah he's a vulgar bird.') ' – the same Little Master, Mr Oliver Vant, Colonel Fortescue, Sir Bradshaw, a – and – ahem – yer's trooly.' (Big was wild.)

Mr Pig rose, & went [to] the rostrum: – 'Your Majesties, Little Master, & gentleman of the – '

'Take tha–at fer said,' broke in Mr Green.

'Turn the bird out!!!' cried the infuriated Little-Master, glad of an opportunity for venting his wrath on the unfortunate parrot.

' – house,' continued Pig calmly. 'I rise to oppose the motion – ' (Cheers. 'Silence!') ' – on the ground that Mr O. Vant & Mr P. Green are unfit to hold office.' (Big – 'Short & poor, boys!')

The Little-Master sent the house into the lobbies & the ballot was passed round. Amid tense excitement they returned & read out 'The motion passes by a majority of 70 votes to 29 votes.' Then in a whisper, 'Now Hawki.'

The sovereign rose & said – 'I do declare the new Clique lawfully to be a Clique in accordance with the laws & customs of the Boxonian government.'

[87]

No sooner had he ceased to speak than a storm of cheering & shouts of 'Long live their Majesties' & 'Long live the new Clique.' Macgoullah alone in the house shouted 'Long live the dismissed Clique!'

As the M.P.'s trooped out Quicksteppe said to Goose 'I'm not sorry, after all.'

THE END

— " I'm not sorrey "—

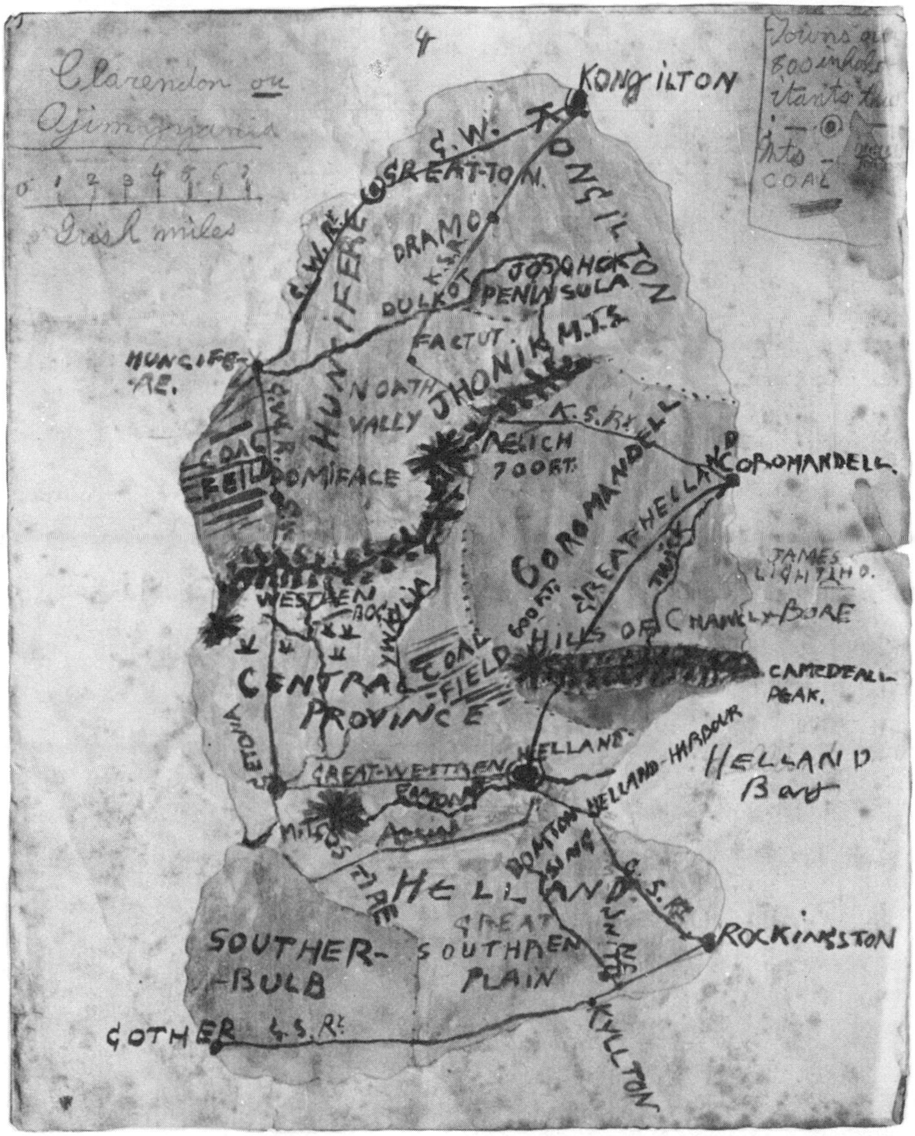

Chapter I

Three months had passed, on the day on which this history opens, since the famous old Clique of Boxen had been broken up to give place to another of younger and more energetic members: and as yet no meeting of this new Clique had been held. Lord Big The Frog, Little Master, detested the new Walterian cabinet and above all all Polonius Green,— a member thereof.

On this particular day, Their Majesties were breakfasting with the Little Master at the Palace Calcutta. The frog appeared more than usually annoyed when they arrived late.

"Upon my word, boys," he exclaimed "I'm

THE LOCKED
DOOR

Sequal to 'Boxen'
& a short sketch entitled
'Than-Kyu'

CHAPTER I

Three months had passed, on the day on which this history opens, since the famous old Clique of Boxen had been broken up to give place to another of younger and more energetic members: and as yet no meeting of this new Clique had been held. Lord Big The Frog, Little Master, detested the new Walterian cabinet and above all Polonius Green, – a member thereof.

On this particular day, Their Majesties were breakfasting with the Little Master at the Palace Calcutta. The frog appeared more than usually annoyed when they arrived late.

'Upon my word, boys,' he exclaimed, 'I'm sick with hunger.'

'We're sorry,' said Benjamin, 'but after all there's no hurry.'

'No hurry?' asked Big. 'Do you know to day is Friday?'

'What about it?' inquired the Rajah.

'Hawki!'

'Big?'

'Dont you remember about the meeting?'

'Oh, it's that disgusting new Clique-meeting!'

'Well let us have some breakfast in the mean time,' suggested Bunny, who was beginning to feel hungry. Acting upon this advice, they all three sat down and adressed themselves with vigour to the eggsoak and curried prauns provided. A curious trio did they form.

The Little Master was a stout frog of massive build, and on the wrong side of 60. His expression was that of a naturally masterful person, given power by exterior circumstances, but slightly pompous & inclined to worrey over small affairs: in appearance he was handsome, and was clad faultlessly in the fashion of 30 years ago. The Rajah was a young man of about 35, happy, careless, and humourous. The rabbit was like his fellow monarch but slightly stouter and not so agile.

After a long pause, the frog observed, 'I could put up with anyone in the Clique except that parrot Polonius Green! An ungentlemanly bird, of moderate faculties, and a set of nasty jokes.'

'I don't like him much myself,' said Bunny, 'but he's very funny at times.'

'Ah, he's very funny at times!!' repeated Lord Big sarcastically. 'If you would only do as I desire & sign a formal objection to the bird, it would be to the point.'

'But my dear Big,' protested the Rajah, 'one can't fly in the face of the country's will.'

'Your fathers,' said Big, 'were kings in the truer sense of the word. The late rajah was not afraid to suspend from the house itself a member he disliked. Benjamin's father was known to do many such things.'

'But in those days – '

'Kings could be men,' vociferated the Little Master with unusual vigour.

'Well,' said the Rajah, 'do I understand that you really object to the fellow?'

'Certainly!'

Big now rose and went out of the breakfast-room. The kings looked at each other: the rabbit spoke.

'Well. Shall we – '

'Lodge a formal objection?'

'To Polonius Green.'

'I think it would create a pleasant excitement.'

'I tell you what: let us see Puddiphat about it.'

Suiting the action to the word, the pair rose and having cast a glance at their morning coats, they walked out into Regency St. After going along this thourafare for some 300 yds. they stopped before 'The Regency' Inn. 'We'll find the Viscount inside,' said the 'jah, and with that they entered.

Lord Big interviewing General Quicksteppe at the latter's residence of *ating House*

CHAPTER II

Leaving the Palace, the Little-Master had stepped into a carriage and driven to the Calcutta house of Lord Quicksteppe, Field-Marshal and ex Clique member. His reasons for paying a visit at this early and consequently unusual hour were multiplex. Firstly he wanted his friend's advice as to what he should do at the meeting of the new Clique. Secondly he wanted to know why on earth he (Quicksteppe) had gone off for a holyday in Clarendon at this crisis.

Arrived before the solid house, he was shown into a salon furnished in the solid splendour and comfort which the old soldier affected. Presently the owner entered: let us observe Field Marshal Frederic Jones Quicksteppe as he is in his 51st year. A tall man of thin once athletic frame, with a flowing brindled beard: a countenance whose noble brow betrayed profound wisdom, while the roguish twinkle in the eyes told that in his laxer moments he might be what is vulgarly termed 'a gay old spark'.

'By dear Big! This is an unexpected pleasure.'

'Good morning. Ah, Quicksteppe what have you been doing abroad?'

'Resting: you seem perturbed.'

'Ah it is this new Clique is bothering me. As you know there [are] many people in it of whom I disaprove. Especially that parrot – Green.'

'Oh: I am sorrey of that.'

'Of course I said to the boys – I mean to the Majesties – that they ought to sign a formal objection to the bird: naturally I don't really mean that they should go so far, but then they don't take any notice.'

'My dear Big,' cried Quicksteppe, 'you've made a fool of yourself.'

'My Lord!!'

'Yes. What if they happen to take you at your word?'

'Ah, indeed there such fellows I never know what they may do!'

'Well, get back to the palace at once & see them. When does the meeting start?'

'At 11.'

'Just time.'

'Good-morning.'

The frog dashed back to his carriage & made what speed he might back to the palace. Here needless to say he did not find them, because they were at the Regency with Puddiphat.

CHAPTER III

When we left them, the two kings had entered the Inner of the Regency, and soon found Viscount Puddiphat, still breaking his fast; this remarkable owl deserves some attention. He was the gayest of all gay Boxonian society, and was reputed to know more about matters sartorial than anyone else alive. He was the proprietor of a large number of eminently successful music-halls called the Alhambras. In appearance he was plump, immaculate, and self-satisfied.

'Good morning your Majesties!' cried the owl. 'I hear you are having your new Clique meeting to day.'

'I blieve so,' said Bunny with a prodigious yawn, 'but by Jove we'll make things hum.'

'Why? Have Your Majesties any scheme on?'

'Scheme!' reiterated the rajah. 'Rather! We are going to formally object to Polonius Green; at least that is what we are thinking of and we came to ask your advice.'

Puddiphat rose & lit a cigar. 'Yes: by all means do so. The bird annoys me by the way he wears his clothes. And as well it will make things move.'

Thanking their friend for his council the two boys decided that, as it was now late, they would go at once to the Clique-meeting. With this intention they directed their steps towards the House of Parliament. Having arrived at the stately pile they entered and came into the robing room, which opened off the Clique-chamber. Here they took of coats & waistcoats preparatory to clothing their bodies in the official emblems of their kingship. Having got this far, Benjamin produced a bottle of Zauber which they both sipped

Sir Chas. Arabudda, Theodore, Mr Reginald Vant, Sir Goose, H.M. The Rajah, General Quicksteppe and Viscount Puddiphat in the Lobby of the House.

[95]

reflectively. Meanwhile Big arrived in the Clique-room outside, and while awaiting his fellow-members heard the kings he desired to warn talking inside the robing-room: here he was in a nice dilemma for no one except the monarchs (according to a venerable custom) was allowed into that apartment.

'Ah, upon my word!' cried the frog beginning to pace up & down the room, 'Its too bad. If I can't get at them before the meeting they're sure to create a scandal over this wretched parrot.'

The other members now began to arrive. First came Oliver Vant, brother to Reginald Vant the Pig. This worthy was a melancholy stockbroker, who, although he had an excellent knowlledge of his own business, was in outer life what vulgar people call a cod. He at once walked up to the already distracted Little-Master, who was still pacing up & down.

'My dear Lord Big, how can I express my delight at seeing that you have adopted Professor Brockenhardt's method of indoor exercise!'

'I beg your pardon Mr Vant!?'

'No not at all, Little Master! True I was the first to adopt this system, but I do not accuse you of plaguerism. In point of fact – '

'My Vant!! Either you are mentally deranged or you have come here for the very purpose of insulting me!'

Fortunately the argument was stopped by the arrival en masse of the other members, Colonel Fortescue, Sir Bradshaw, and Polonius Green.

Fortescue was an army man, who also kept some music halls. Bradshaw was an able barrister and competent politician. Polonius Green as we know was a small ship owner. There also entered the usher, a lugubrious tortoise. The 2 kings now appeared looking very uncomfortable in robes & crowns. Before them the usher bore the double crown of Boxen, in addition to their individual circlets. Benjamin spoilt everything by entering with his set at a racy angle: at a look, however, from the Little-Master he restored it to a horizontal position. As the party seated themselves round the table, Big made frantic but useless efforts to whisper in the Rajah's ear. Finding this unfeasable he at last addressed the Clique.

'Your Majesties, and Gentlemen: the business of the Clique to day is Mr Green's motion, the purport of which he has not thought fit to reveal. I request him to speak.'

The bird rose. 'Yer Majesties, Little Master and Gents.' (At this juncture Big said to their majesties in an aside 'Ah, he's poor, poor!') 'The motion

South Dolfin-Land and the Tracities

I purpose is that there should be a Chessman in this Clique.' (Big who abominated the Chessmen as aliens gave a start.) 'Considering the number of Chessmen in the country and the positions they hold, it is only fair that they should sit in the Clique. The advantages fer this are too obvious to pint out, so I'll say no more.'

Big rose. 'Your Majesties, and Gentlemen' (with much stress on the last word – at this point Polonius broke in 'Gents, Gents, m'lord, much shorter.' – 'Keep the bird quiet usher!' roared Big in fury. 'In answer to Mr Green's proposal I say that Chessmen are aliens, nothing more: if indeed they hold high positions, they should not.'

Polonius broke in. 'M'lord, ye'd do better not to say much about aliens. Because, yer one yerself, not fergetting you come from the dependant island of Piscia, which is only a colony, all said & done.'

For a whole minute the frog stood paralysed with an ungovernable fury. Then taking from his pocket a handkerchief, he flipped the bird in the face, saying as he did so, 'Meet me on the Bumregis road with what weapons you like at 3 to morrow morning.'

CHAPTER IV

For nearly 3 minutes intense silence hung over the Clique. The Rajah & Bunny gave a faint giggle, Mr Vant mournfully shook his head at Green, Bradshaw coughed, and Lord Big stood still in his rage: the only person who appeared absoloutly at his ease was Polonius Green, who presently broke the silence by saying, '3 in the morning My Lord, is an hour when all sober and respectable citizens have retired. If you are still gadding about at that time, that's no reason fer expec'ing others to join you in vulgar brawls.'

This disgraceful speech left every other member of the Clique absolutely astounded: the Little-Master had by this time however sufficiently collected his faculties to reply in these words:

'Your Majesties, and Gentlemen, Mr Green has accused me of being an alien as a native of Piscia. I could defend myself from this charge, – were I so inclined –, on the gound that I was born in Mouseland, and educated at Danphabel School, never even seeing Piscia untill my twentyeth year. But, Gentlemen, I will not call this up in my defence, because it is the greatest regret of my life that I was not born in my native land, a land of

Ruins of the first united Boxonian Parliament
House in Piscia

which its sons are justly proud as their fatherland. Those of you who know
ancient history will remember that the Empire of Piscia was civilized and
powerful under its emperor Pau-Amma, 200 years before the Pongeeins
invaded Animalland and reduced it to their crude order. In more modern
times Piscia is still as brilliant as in the old days. Was she not honoured by
being the seat of the first united Parliament of Boxen? And why, do you
think was it chosen to be such? Doubtless our feathered friend would tell
us, "Because it was part of neither country & therefore favoured neither."
But no, a thousand times no. It was because it was part of both countries
& therefore favoured both equally. This island gave birth to Little-Master
White, a frog, perhaps the greatest Little Master ever seen by Boxen. Does
Mr Green, knowing as he ought to the greatness of Piscia, call me an alien?
I do not remonstrate on account of the insult offered to me, but on account
of the dirt thrown by a bird on the hitherto clean escutcheon of one of
Boxen's most important states.

'Gentlemen, if I have wandered somewhat from the actual subject of this
debate, I crave your pardon, only pleading as my excuse the human weak-

ness of not being able to sit by and calmly submit to the dastardly insults this member was heaping on me, on my countrymen, & worst of all on Piscia herself. To return to this same member's motion that Chessmen should sit in the Clique: – Mr Green speaks of the high positions held by this homeless nation of restless vagabonds. I grant you, Mr Green, that Chessmen do hold important offices, but you will grant me that they have been elected to the same by the country. This same country is so used to seeing these aliens in places that should be their own that they fail to realise the monstrous wrong and injustices of it all: so they vote for Chessmen blithely, but not credit to the aliens themselves. Let us sift the matter to the bottom! Who are these Chess? They are a nation without a country, a people without a king, a mighty force without a standing army. Yes! Without a country yet every country in the world is theirs. They live in this land, they do not pay our taxes but they are protected by our laws. They collect money, and give nothing in return. Oh!, have they not enough unmerited privileges, that you would add this one thing more.'

A storm of furious applause shook the Clique Room as the old frog sat down. All eyes naturally turned to the parrot to see what affect the speech had had upon him: he sat with ruffled feathers in one corner glaring at his opponent. No sentiment of the grandeur of the defence influenced him, no shame for his behaviour. Only annoyance at the failure of his motion.

At this juncture Benjamin rose & said, 'Whereas, we the kings of Boxen, do hereby lodge a formal objection against Polonius Green Esquire, he is no longer a member of the Clique.'

CHAPTER V

To the Little Master, as we have seen, Chessmen were an abomination, as a class. But he was sensible enough not to condemn individual Chess whom he really liked. And none did he like better than Samuel Macgoullah, a knight. This worthy was not a member of Boxonian city society, but he was before everything a gentlemen. Although he dressed in a pea-jacket, although he spoke with a strong Murry accent, although he went to the pit in theatres & took a gladstone-bag full of oranges, although he captained his own little schooner the Bosphorous, Macgoullah was a gentleman. True, some snobs did not recognize the fact because when he became rich and an

M.P. he still lived as he always had done. On the evening after the meeting of the new Clique, he would have been found sitting in the Inner of the Schooner Inn (a homely & comfortable hostelry in the docks) with 2 friends.

Meeting of friends in 'the Schooner.'

One of these was Mr Green, and the other needs some comment. He was a bear clad in the uniform of a naval chief steward, or as he liked to call it 'purser'. He was short and inclined to corpulence, good-humoured, and self-satisfied: in fact he was Jas. Bar Purser of H.M. gunboat Thrush. One cannot say more!

Green was talking to both loudly. 'This d—d toad, & these two fellows ye call kings have had the impudence to turn me out of their Clique.'

'Never mind, Polonius,' said Macgoullah consolingly, 'its no great loss.'

Bar had been one of the many who had tried 3 months ago to get a place in the new Clique, but without success: consequently he had no sympathy with the bird.

''Pon my word Green,' he cried, 'your hard to please. You've been in the Clique for 3 months, & I havn't had a day! But I'm not making a song about it.'

'Three months, you little scugy! And only had one meeting.'

'Ah well,' put in Macgoullah, 'the only thing to do is to try & get another Clique formed.'

'Billocks!! I want personal revenge on the toad & his 2 young friends – '

'No!' shouted the Chessknight, 'Not a word against their majesties, they've always been good friends to me.'

'Lot of use their friendship to *you* is to *me*, you sloppy mule! But I'll go for the toad!'

'A duel?' said Bar.

'A duel,' said the bird with scorn, 'what d'ye take me fer? No, some little scheme: think of something.'

Bar was silent for some seconds & then cried 'I have it,' & burst into laughter.

'What is it?'

But Bar only rocked to & from with aching sides & streaming eyes.

'What is it?' reiterated his friends. At last when Bar was able to explain his plan all 3 began a hearty guffaw at the scheme. It was as follows: to buy (at the Little-Master's expence) 500 golf balls, with which they would (by the connivance of the palace servants) stuff his matress: if the plan was not sanguinary enough to suit Green, he at any rate kept that view to himself.

At this moment a servant entered and handed envelopes to Bar and Macgoullah: tearing his open the latter found the following missive: –

It is not everyone who is invited to a royal ball so our worthy Macgoullah was pleased. Bar's was the same & they both announced the fact.

Green was annoyed.

CHAPTER VI

Great was the preparation of Bar and Macgoullah when the eventful evening arrived. Bar had hired a handsome to be ready for them both outside the 'Schooner' where they had arranged to meet.

As they drew near the palace, Regency Street became a mass of moving lights dancing to the music of horses' hoofs and the powerful purr of motors: and it was not without difficulty that the hireling Jehu navigated them to the portals of Regency St Palace. Stepping out they were conducted by suave domestics to the cloak room, which, as is usually the case on these occasions, was crowded with knots of whispering guests fiddling with their gloves. There of course is Puddiphat immaculately clad; there is Reginald Pig the Shipowner dressed in solid and plain evening dress; there is Quick-steppe looking finer than ever as the electric light catches his glossy curling locks; there is Colonel Chutney, formerly head of the war office, but now removed to give place to Fortescue who is also present. After some time of nervous fumbling and brushing, Pig, the most couragious person present, led a sort of forlorn hope to the salon where their Majesties were recieving their guests and where stout domestics dispensed tea etc. The two kings were throwing all their histrionic powers into an imitation of enjoyment, and behind them stood the Little-Master looking rather worried. The boys kept up a continual flow of conversation: –

'Good evening, My dear Pig! How are the ships? Ah, Viscount Puddiphat, very glad you came.'

'Good evening Your Majesties. Ah my dear Little-Master I see you've been having busy times in the Clique.'

'Yes,' said Big drily.

The Duchess of Penzly came up, a heavy woman whom they all abominated.

'Good evening Duchess. Hasn't Miss Penzly – oh! Influenza? I am very sorry to hear that.' The Duchess passed on to Big. 'Ah, Lord Big, this is a pleasure. How delighted I was to hear you had had some excitement in politics, it does liven things up so, doesn't it?'

'It certainly does,' responded the frog brusquely, and engaged a dance.

Little Bar now came up. The boys turned to him.

'Good evening Mr Bar. Hot, isn't it? It has been all day. Good evening Miss Eglington, I don't think you've met Mr Bar. Allow me – Miss Eglington – Mr Bar: Mr Bar – the hon. Miss Eglington.' Bar moved off dutifully to engage a dance, which he did.

'Have you seen "The Three Looneys"?' inquired Bar.

'Yes. What did you think of it?'

'Excellent. Of course the caricature of their Majesties and the Little-Master was rather obvious.'

'Oh yes, but I don't think they will take any offence.'

'Not their Majesties but Lord Big may.'

The music now struck up the opening bars of the first waltz, and the actual dancing began. A detailed description of that famous evening would be tedious, so let it suffice to say that it was a great success, in spite of the fact that Big's every partner mentioned the recent political rupture. True, one lady, gazing at the frog's somewhat out of date costume, observed, 'I wish I had known it was fancy dress, Little-Master: you quite remind one of the dear old times!'

At 3, all the guests having departed, our 3 friends were able to retire to their bedrooms. Lord Big, thoroughly tired lost no time in undressing and throwing himself on his bed.

What was that? Surely it hardly seemed as softly carressing as usual! And why was it so springy under him: it seemed to be entirely made of hard round balls! Perhaps it was only fancy, so he gallantly lay there for ten minutes. Then he could stand it no longer. The pain, – no other word was adequate – the pain was too intolerable. Wiping his brow he gazed at the couch of torment. Drawing a heavy sigh he began to pace the room. In the dead of night the time went slowly, and he decided he couldn't walk about till dawn. He bent over the matress & examined it: he could not conceive what was the matter, so, with really wonderful fortitude, he decided to make another attempt. But in three minutes he leapt from the bed. He would not stand it, he told himself, he would open the matress, & diagnose the cause of the trouble. Drawing a pocket-knife he made a large slit in the envelope & shook it. A second later he regreted the rash act for a deluge of golf-balls sprang out, bouncing from floor to walls and thence to the Little-Master's person: ball after ball rushed on its headlong course of glancing. Accidently placing his foot on one, it shot from under him & through his mirror. At that moment, Benjamin entered, attracted by the unusual noise, to behold the little master ankle deep in balls and dodging a regular whirlwind of the same.

'Hullo, Big!' he exclaimed, 'What ever *are* you doing?'

CHAPTER VII

Polonius Green! Ah! Perhaps the reader has wondered concerning the manner of this bird's life. With whom did he concert? who were his friends? where was his residence? He mixed gladly with anyone he could: he was despised by the greater part of society, as 'novus homo'. Yet many of the best people attended his breakfasts & suppers. Who were they? – People like Puddiphat who could get on with anyone: distinct from this class was the admiring crowd who toadied to his wealth.

On the morning after the royal ball, he was giving a select breakfast party at his town residence of Shelling House: the guests were Reginald Pig, Puddiphat, Bar, & Macgoullah. Pig came because he & Green were both shipowners and had common topics of interest in business matters. Puddiphat came because Green's cellar was good. He never disguised the fact to his host, and the parrot himself was in too much awe of the viscount to resent it: the owl with almost brutal frankness censured or commended Green's costume and conversation: in fine he took Green in hand and ruled him with a rod of iron, which the latter brooked with a meekness really remarkable in one usually so peppery. The other 2 of course came as old friends. Green was in great form.

'Jolly glad you all came,' he said. 'Do you see they've chucked me from their Clique?'

'Yes,' said Pig, 'but now-a-days no one is in the Clique.'

'In fact,' said the owl, 'I should not wonder if in two or three months none of the best people *would* go into the Clique.'

'Then,' replied Polonius, 'take it fer gra-anted I'll keep out.'

'Green,' said the viscount severely, 'you are not one of the best people, and do not affect to give up the idea of a Cliqueship!!'

'Sorry 'phat: I only meant it was more trouble than it was worth.'

'Anyway,' said Macgoullah, 'things are so changeable now that the Clique is not the same for a fortnight together.'

'By the way,' said Bar (who since his unsuccessful attempt to enter the Clique had lost all interest in politics), 'I wonder how Big slept last night.'

'What's that wheeze?' inquired Pig. It was just being related, when a servant entered and handed Pig a large letter. It was from the Frater Senior of the Tracity Chessary (the senior Chessary of the world) & ran thus: –

> Dear Sir,
>
> Having considered the best policy to adopt in foreign trade, we are come to the decision that it is best to place it entirely in the hands of one company. Whereas we are decided that the best company for this pur-pose is the Green Line, we have no further use of your services.
>
> Signed 身丁ṙ;ᛉ (Frater Senior Tracit. 66.)
>
> Nov 20-12.

'Ah,' thought Pig. 'Now we know why our parrot was so keen on the Chess seats in the Clique.'

Aloud he said, 'Gentlemen, read this.'

The letter was passed round, and as each guest mastered its contents, he turned his eyes on the parrot, who sat in alarm, knowing well what the missive was. Like one man they rose & strode silently from the room. Puddiphat was last to go, & Green spoke to him.

'Er, Puddles, old bird, what are they all going fer?'

The owl turned round and gave Polonius one long steady look, then turned & went, shutting the door after him.

Metaphorically too he shut the door.

[106]

CHAPTER VIII

The two Vant brothers, were known by all Calcutta. The eldest, Oliver Vant, had been brought up in great ease by his parents and was an excellent stockbroker. His brother Reginald, the Pig, had gone to sea as a boy and finally had become Shipowner in partnership with Bradley. Their business relations had soon been supplement by a firm private friendship, and so the three lived together at Murry in Ferdis Hall, and at Calcutta in Mnason House.

After leaving Shelling House, Reginald went to his office to find a note from Bradley saying that the latter had taken a half-day off: stepping into

Rupture between Visc. Puddiphat & Mr. Green, at Shelling House

a handsome he gave the order to drive to Mnason House. In 15 minutes he drew up before the door and entered. In the study he found Bradley ensconced in an armchair before the fire.

'Hullo Reggie, you look annoyed.'

'Annoyed! A terrible thing has happenned.'

'What?'

'Green!!'

'"Green has happened"? What do you mean?'

'He has – but this letter will explain all,' said Pig producing the missive from the Frater Senior of the Tracity. Bradley read it.

'D—n the bird,' he said slowly, 'What do you purpose to do?'

'I don't know. Of course he has obviously been bribed with this privilege, but one cannot prove it.'

'One can have a try. Our trade with the Tracities is quite a large fraction of our total.'

'Yes. I gave everyone his letter to read, and they'll all cut him after this.'

'What a fool you are, Reggie! Who cares whether they cut him or not, when we've lost the Tracities?'

'He does.'

'Rot. And if he does, that doesn't give us the Tracities.'

'No-o. We ought to speak to someone in authority about it.'

'Yes: it could do no harm, anyhow. The Little-Master might do.'

'No, no. General Quicksteppe is a far more capable man!'

'Yes, but he holds no office now.'

'Well, he could get Big to carry out his plans.'

'Perhaps, Reggie, but the frog is one who always thinks his own plans best.'

'Well shall I speak to him in person?'

The other was silent for a moment.

'But what do you suppose any of them could do?'

'I don't know: but they might do some good & they could do no harm.'

'Very well then, Reggie. When can you see the frog?'

'I tell you what. Their Majesties told me last night that he and they were going to see "The 3 Looneys" at Oxenham's. Let's go to night & I can speak to him in his box.'

'Very well. And, we'll see the play at the same time.'

'Yes. I'll bring Olly.'

At this moment the elder Vant arrived from his office. Oliver Vant had often been called a gloomy misanthrope but this was unjust. He was an excellent man in his own business, and in private life kindly though pompous.

'Good evening Reginald,' said Oliver, 'you are early at home.'

'Yes, Olly. Bradley & I are going to Oxenham's to night, will you come?'

It was the custom of the 3 to play whist every evening, and Oliver prefered it to a musical-comedy.

'Reginald, we will play whist.'

'Oh no Olly.'

'Reginald!! However I will come.'

So after an early dinner, they entered their car, and drove to the theatre.

CHAPTER IX

On this Friday evening Oxenham's theatre was crowded with spectators of every rank, anxious to see 'The three Looneys'. This play was written round 3 characters, a hare, a negro, and a toad, all more or less obvious charactures of Benjamin, the Rajah and the Little-Master. It could never have been produced in any country where the king was not so good-humoured and careless as 'the boys': some fear was felt by Mr Putney (the manager) as to how the Little-Master would view it. In any case he was coming and one could but hope for the best; in the meantime he had an excellent house. There sat Quicksteppe in his box, prepared to thoroughly enjoy himself, as, indeed, he usually was. There in the opposite box was Goose, the eminent barrister, gazing round the house. There in another was our friend the viscount, as immaculate as ever, & sharing the box with him was Colonel Chutney. In the dress-circle sat the two Vants and Bradley: not far from them was Fortescue, head of the war-office. There in the stalls was Bar, and his fellow officers off his gunboat. In the pit sat Green, in that humble part because having lost his social standing, he saw no reason to throw away money by going elsewhere. Also in the pit we would have found honest Macgoullah, well fortified by a gladstone-bag of oranges. The orchestra presently appeared and began the overture, and shortly after its commencement the door of the royal box opened and the Little-Master, Hawki and Benjamin entered, greeted by loud cheers from all parts of the house.

"The Three Looneys" at Oxenham's

'Ah,' said Bunny sitting down, 'thats a good house.'

'Aye rather;' said the frog, 'if the play is proportionally good it'll be all right.'

By this time the overture had come to a noisy end, and the curtain rose upon the first act.

The plot was roughly as follows: 'Large', the toad falls in love with an actress and on requiring admission to her house is refused it by the porter ('Will'um') unless he pays £500. After some discussion by the three, Large is left alone on the stage and attempts to climb up through the window & is repulsed. At the end of the act he gets the money by raffling the vacant office of censorship, which Will'um wins.

When the curtain fell the Little-Master was furious.

'Ah there's a libel action in every line. I won't stand it.'

'Oh Big!!' exclaimed Hawki, 'its splendid. It characitures us just as much, but we don't mind.'

'No,' echoed Bunny, 'Its all right Big, you're too easily offended.'

'It may be very funny Benjamin but no playright should bring scorn and discredit on those who ought to be looked upon as the pillars of the state.'

'But,' rejoined the rabbit, 'it doesn't bring "scorn & discredit" on us. Anyway I'm going over to have a chat with Puddiphat: coming 'Jah?'

The Rajah eagerly assented to this proposal and the two monarchs strolled across to the Viscount's box.

'Good evening Majesties', cried the owl, 'and how is our respected Little-Master receiving the play?'

'Badly. He is rather annoyed.'

'Really? Hullo,' said Chutney glancing across at the royal box, 'Old Reggie Vant is having a crack with him.'

At this point the bustle in the orchestra seemed to betoken a second rise of the curtain and the kings returned to their own box to find Lord Big in a state of great consternation. So engrossed were they in his tale of what the pig had told him that they hardly observed the second act at all: this fortunately was not vital to the plot as it included merely Large's adventures on the stage, which he takes up to be near his lover. The act ended in a burlesque three-cornered fight between the three looneys. Loud and vociferous applause shook Oxenham's at the fall of the curtain on the second act and Miss Leroy as the actress, Peter Bhül as Large and Philias Dugge as

Will'um were called before the curtain to the intense satisfaction of Alexander Putney.

'Well,' said the frog at the end of the act, 'I don't see whats to be done about that parrot. You put me in a nasty hole by lodging that objection, but now I'm glad you did. Vant, as you know, is furious about it & has appealed to me. Ah, really its hard to know what to do. The bribery is obvious but there is no proof.'

'Call a Clique-meeting on the subject,' sugested Hawki.

Big was silent: he did not want to meet his Clique again. He did not yet feel sure how they would regard Green's expulsion, for which he was considered directly responsible, and although it would have been very unjust to say that he was afraid of meeting his Clique he certainly regarded it as a disagreeable duty which might be put off indefinetly: in his heart of hearts he hoped that it would die a natural death before it met again, and a new one would take its place.

In the pit Macgoullah, now full of joy and oranges, was praising the new play up to the skies, while Bar and his friends in the stalls pronounced it excellent. The curtain now rose on the third and last act, in which Large comes to the heroine's door with his bribe for Will'um. The latter however, on becoming censor, has given over porterdom, & the new one knows nothing about the bargain. The heroine at last appears and each of the three Looneys propose to her in turn, in a series of beautiful duets, & all are refused. In the end she marries Will'um & the three go on as before. The finale to this third act was encored time after time, and even the lugubrious Oliver Vant admitted that he had enjoyed himself.

But for the kings & the Little-Master the evening had not been very gay, for the latter was gloomy & upset by his disturbing news & the others were affected by his gloom. Green retired to Shelling House in good spirits, and as he ate his supper looked at the picture of himself on the opposite wall.

'Ah,' he thought, 'they've cut me now, but I'm not done fer: of course it would have been pleasant in society, but this has its 'vantages. Now I can dress as I like, & not mind what Puddiphat says. Eh?'

CHAPTER X

For a long period after they went to see 'The Three Looneys' their Majesties led an uneventful and blameless life, and Lord Big left politics strictly alone. The pile of letters on his desk recieved each morning a more cursory glance, and those that urgently needed a reply recieved as short a one as possible: indeed for nearly a month he was seldom seen outside Regency St Palace. But the nation was keen on politics at this time and voices were heard to say everywhere 'that one insolent parrot should not upset Boxonian shipping'. For the loss of trade with the Tracities was a grave one, and not to be put up with.

Big was as honestly annoyed about this as anyone, but he knew that he could do nothing by himself, and, as we have seen, yet dreaded a Clique-meeting. This state of affairs could not go on for ever, and he realised this suddenly when he heard a tubthumping orator in a back street one day crying 'We'll have a meeting not only of the Clique but also of the Parliament, despite this lazy frog.' He went home in high dudgeon, but next night, while at dinner with Quicksteppe, an indiscreet guest said in his hearing that 'the Clique wouldn't stand this much longer'.

Their Majesties, of course were only too glad to escape what was to them an indescribable bore: the news of the anger of the country against Green and against the Chess was for them a topic of conversation and not a vital question to be grappled with.

On a Saturday morning some five weeks after their visit to Oxenham's, the three had finished their breakfast and were sitting in the palace smoking room. A servant announced that the Clique members were in the ante-room & wished to see their Majesties and the Little-Master.

So the blow had fallen!

'Come on boys,' said Big, bracing his nerves for the ordeal. They entered a large reception room and required the guests to enter. The Clique members entered and bowed to the kings. Big noticed with relief that Green was not there, – they had recognized the objection formaly so nothing more could be said about it, the matter was closed.

Fortescue, who appeared to be their leader, stood forth an said, 'Your Majesties, and Little-Master, I crave pardon for interrupting you at this

unusual [hour], but the matter on which I come will brook no procrastina-
tion – '

'Then hurry up with it!!' broke in the Little-Master whose nervousness
rendered him irritable.

' – Yes, Little-Master, with your kind attention. There having now been
no meeting of the Clique for over a month – '

'None was required,' said Big.

'But Little-Mà – '

'If the Little-Master says so, so it is,' said Oliver Vant in the tone of a
judge pronouncing death sentence.

'Hold your tongue, Vant,' said Fortescue hotly. 'You came here to agitate
for a meeting & now you fly in our faces.'

'Come, come, Gentlemen!' said Big, 'No brawling in the Presence!!'

'To continue,' said Fortescue wearily, 'we the members of the Clique
demand at once a meeting – '

'No we don't,' said Oliver Vant dolefully.

'But I thought – '

'Ah me! So did I. But the Little-Master's silent influence has turned me.
He, as I know does not wish a meeting, and the dumb eloquence of his
personality has – '

'Very well, very well,' said Fortescue hastily, 'Well Your Majesties we
(excepting Mr Vant) desire at once a meeting of the Clique on the question
of Mr Green's (Big began to fidget) alliance with the Tracities against our
shipping world. Rê this I may say – '

' – Nothing at present,' said the Rajah to everyone's surprise. 'In the
meeting to morrow you may say anything.' The rajah had not done so much
ruling on his own for years, and when he looked at Bunny to see if he
agreed, that worthy rabbit was too surprised to make any sign.

Encouraged by this, Hawki went on 'Unless you have anything more to
demand the audience is closed.'

'Hawki,' whispered Big in his ear, 'will you leave these things to me?'

'One thing more,' said Fortescue, 'The vacancy created in the Clique by
the expulsion (Big looked uncomfortable) of Mr Polonius Green must be
replaced. The members have unanimously agreed to Mr Alexander Putney,
and we beg Your Majesties' consent.'

'What?' cried Big, 'The manager of a theatre which produces plays written against its sovereigns? Do you purpose to confer upon this immoral man

of histrionic gains the honour of a Cliqueship?'

'My Lord,' said Bunny taking his cue from his fellow-monarch's recent boldness, 'your vote cannot outweigh those of the whole Clique, which is still unanimous, (Oliver Vant opened his mouth to speak but the other members got in front of him) so we are pleased to admit Mr Alexander Putney to our Clique.'

'So are we,' said the Rajah.

'The audience is ended,' said Bunny.

The Clique-members, with many bows and genuflections left the room, and the boys heaved sighs of relief.

Big said, 'I wish you'd leave things to me more on these occasions.'

CHAPTER XI

On Monday morning at 10 o.c., the second meeting of the Clique was held. Big and their Majesties were there early, and the latter retired to their robing room leaving the frog sitting anxiously in the luxurious little cabinet. The first member to arrive was Fortesque, who was as bright and vigorous as usual.

'Good morning, my dear Little-Master, we have what is likely to prove a very important meeting before us.'

'Every Clique-meeting is important,' replied Big. 'But why this especially?'

'Because, My Lord, this Chess question is rather serious.'

At this point Alexander Putney, the new member, arrived. He was a short spare man, with an energetic cleanshaven face, and was clad in a morning-coat that even the viscount would not have been ashamed to wear.

'Good day, My Lord,' said he, 'these are new grounds for us to meet upon.'

'Yes,' replied the Little-Master somewhat tersely, for, as we have seen, he did not entirely approve of his new fellow Cliqueman.

At this juncture, our friend the melancholy tortoise announced, 'Mr Vant, & Sir Bradshaw.'

'Ah,' said Big, 'We are all here I think. Theodore (for so the tortoise was named) go and see if it is Their Majesties' pleasure to enter.'

Theodore dissapeared into the robing room and soon returned bearing the double crown of Boxen on a cushion and followed by Benjamin and the Rajah.

As soon as all were seated, Lord Big cleared his throat and began, 'Your Majesties and Gentlemen, you, the members of this Clique, have gone through the irregular proceeding of demanding a Clique-meeting: I therefore suppose that you have some important motion to propose, and I request whomsoever is your leader to speak on your behalf.'

Fortescue rose up at once.

'Your Majesties, Little-Master, and Gentlemen: we are met here to day for the purpose of discussing what steps ought to be taken in the interest of Boxonian commerce, which, as you know, is at this time greatly imperilled by the Chess. The suspicious and the malicious have connected Polonius Green's efforts to gain for these Chess seats in this Clique with the sole right of trade which Frater Senior Von Quinklë conferred upon him. About the truth of these statements I know nothing. Our present question is what we can do to defend our other shipowners against these Chess. And, Gentlemen, I feel sure that the nation will yield to no persuasion. I propose, therefore, that a message be sent to Von Quinklë demanding that he withdraw his trade edict: if he agrees, the matter is closed: but if he refuses there is only one remedy – war!'

The state of the Clique room was what the papers describe as 'sensation'. Big was the first to speak.

'Your Majesties, and Gentlemen; war is a great and in this case not absolutely necessary expense of lives and money. Nevertheless I think that Field Marshal Fortescue's suggestion of writing to Von Quinklë is excellent. But war is too great a thing to be decided by the Clique, we must have a meeting of the whole Parliament.'

'Hear, Hear,' cried several people who were anxious to shift the reponsability onto other shoulders.

'Well,' continued the Little-Master, 'does eveyone agree to writing to Von Quicklë? Theodore, pass round the ballot.'

After a breathless two minutes of borrowing pencils and gaining paper, the tortoise read out 'For the motion 4. Against the motion 1.'

Every one glanced at his neighbour as if to ask who the culprit was. Oliver Vant shook his head mournfully from side to side, muttering, 'They have all voted for it. Oh dear!!'

Accordingly a letter was drawn up and signed by Benjamin and the Rajah.

Eight days later Big called the Clique together again, and read them his reply, which ran as follows: –

To The Little Master of Dozen:–
Sir;
   we received your document, containing a demand for us to cease to do that which is our right. And, whereas, we have already issued a decree concerning this shipping, we refuse to withdraw the said decree. And, moreover, we do hereby urge you to give up all idea of persuading us to alter our opinions either by molestation or by argument.
                signed 𝔉ⁱ.Ɉ.𝔉ⁱ (Frater Senior)
                                    Fraed. Co.

Jan. 3. ˜13.

The Clique, even including Oliver Vant, was furious at such an unconditional refusal, and that very afternoon notices were put up in Calcutta that a meeting of the Parliament would be held on the following day. That afternoon as they sat in the palace garden, Big said to the boys, 'Ah, you know, there won't be any war.'

'Why,' said Bunny, 'Won't the Parliament agree?'

'Yes, I expect they will: but when we get to the scene of action it will fizzle out.'

'Oh rot,' said Hawki.

'Hawki!!' cried Big reprovingly, 'Don't talk like that: anyway we're sure to have to go to the Tracities, whether there'll be anything to do when we get there or not. As we'll be away for some time I'll just look through last year's bills & get things settled.'

With this laudable object in view the worthy frog left his soverigns and

[117]

strolled into his office. Everything seemed alright till his eyes lit on the last item of his 'Private Expenses' bill.

Seeing this he nearly fainted.

It was –

500 . . . Golf balls at 2s each . . . £50.

'Ah, I won't pay it,' muttered the irate Little-Master. 'It's that fellow who stuffed my matress: I'll get him yet.'

CHAPTER XII

Calcutta was considerably surprised by the announcement of a coming meeting of Parliament, but this surprise was on the whole agreeable, for the country had begun to tire of its long imposed rest from politics. On the morning of the meeting, Viscount Puddiphat sat in 'The Regency', having a glass of Zauber with Reginald Vant.

'On the whole, Reggie,' said he, 'I'm glad about this meeting: the Parliament bar supplies some of the best Vin de Brus I ever drank.'

'Yes,' replied the other, 'and it'll be a jolly exciting session too.'

The owl was not vastly interested in the political aspect of the session. However he said, 'How so?'

'There may be war. My brother Olly – '

'War with whom?'

'The Chess, of course: you might know that.'

'By the way, if we're going to turn up, we'd better start now.'

'Right. Come along.'

The Calcutta 'House' was a massive building of imposing appearance. Passing through a stone vestibule, the two friends proceeded along a wide corridor and entered the actual council-chamber, a large and lofty hall capable of seating 500 members. At one end, on a raised dais stood the double throne and between its two compartments the Little-Master's chair: these three seats were at present empty. The benches, which ran down either side parallel and were five deep, were only half-full, and other members were arriving through the great double-flanged doors. The viscount nodded to Samuel Macgoullah and wended his way to his alloted seat, leaving the Pig to do likewise. After about quarter of an hour's wait, during which time the spectators' gallery filled, a loud gong was rung without for silence; all conversation ceased and in a few seconds a hitherto fast closed door opened and a small procession entered. First came Sir Charles Arrabudda, royal bearer of the sceptre, clutching in his hands an enormous engine of gold, which the house knew instinctively to be the sceptre. Next came Colonel Chutney, State Herald, bearing a fearsome & antiquated sound-producer. Then came Theodore bearing the double crown on a chusion: this worthy tortoise was followed by the Clique-members. After these came their Majesties in robes & coronets: and the rear was brought up [by] the Frog.

When everyone was seated, Chutney stood forth and raised the trumpet to his lips. Now we do not attempt to account for what happened, for Chutney is a good man and his enemies are few. The eyes of the Boxonian Parliament were fixed on him as his cheeks slowly swelled out with air, and all nerves were braced to bear the blast: one or two musical members got up and tiptoed out: an old lady in the gallery put her fingers to her ears. – But no sound came!! The Colonel took the trumpet from his mouth and shook it: then he had another try which proved quite as abortive as the first. Chutney got slightly red and blew harder: but for two minutes, as he stood there with shaking knees and scarlet inflated cheeks, silence reigned supreme. At last the unfortunate man muttered an inaudible announcement and dashed to his bench. Years after he discovered that Polonius Green had filled his instrument with glue.

The Little-Master rose and walked to the rostrum. In a concise speech he told the house the state of affairs and informed them that [the] question was 'war or peace?'

Mr Vant said that it was foolish to send the army to the Tracities when the Chess in Boxen might rise as soon as they (the troops) were gone.

Fortescue pointed out with some heat that they need not send the whole army to the Tracities.

Sir Charles Arrabudda explained the necessity of gaining the Tracity trade – an interesting fact which had been taken for granted at the very start. He went on in his soothing musical voice to draw a picture of the islands which lasted 2 hours and a half.

The Little-Master said that if they submitted to this treatment (he meant from the Chessary not from Sir Chas.) no nation would respect them.

Mr Green moved that the ballot be passed round.

Mr R. Vant advocated war, but said that the Chess would probably capitulate as soon as they (the Boxonians) arrived.

Mr Macgoullah denied this.

Mr Green moved that the ballot be passed round.

This time The Little-Master agreed, and the house retired to the lobbies.

In a few minutes the counting was over and Big read out, 'For war 368.' (Loud cheers.) 'Against 132: majority ah – er – er' (Big was a poor arithmetician) '336.'

CHAPTER XIII

Although the Tracity islands could only muster some 3 thousand inhabitants a fairly large expedition was fitted out against them. The Little-Master who had fought many a battle in his younger days was full of joy at the idea of entering on another campaign. He called, of course, a Clique meeting on the subject and therein asked Fortescue, who (it will be remembered) was head of the war office, to state his plans. It was finally decided that the government should commandeer the Star liner *Indian Star* as a troopship, a single screw steamer of 7654 tons register. The Gunboat *Thrush*, of which our old friend Bar was purser, was also to go: she was also a single screw vessel of 568 tons. Also the *Cygnet*, a small but very neat & useful steamer of 98 tons, the private yacht of their Majesties. The 'Chutneys', under command of Colonel Chutney, and the 'Mouselands' a semi-volunteer regiment under command of Puddiphat, who ranked as a corporal, were ordered to the front. This latter regiment, being composed of voluntary recruits, naturally varied in size, but on this occasion several volunteers had to be refused admission as it was already full.

The effect of these warlike preparations on Polonius Green was disturbing. The Chess, who had bribed him, would in all probability give him away if the war went against them, and he would thus stand convicted of bribery.

He realised these facts as he was strolling with a cigar on his roof-garden at Shelling House.

'D—n it, this alliancing with foreigners is a mistaek. Some years ago I very near ruined meself by puttin' me head in the noose of some Prussians. But here I go again. Well, I shan't get left again: not good enough fer Polonius Green. I have it.'

With that he went below and produced a sheet of note-paper. Taking up a pen he wrote: –

'Ah,' he thought, 'I'll not be a fool fer to send it through the post jest now. With a war on letters to Von Quin – Von Quin – Von – er – the Frater Senior will look suspicious.' He then placed a hat on his head & walked to the docks where he sought out one of his own boats & committed the letter to her captain.

Late in the afternoon on which the expedition started, their Majesties were sitting in their smoke-room entirely forgetful of it, when the Little-Master, clad in the full Field Marshal's uniform which as a member of the staff he was entitled to wear, burst in upon them.

'Boys, have you not changed into your uniforms yet? The boats start in an hour.'

'So they do,' cried Bunny. 'Come on 'Jah, no time to spare.'

With feverish haste the two monarchs dashed to their rooms, and after a superhuman exertion of their protean skill re-appeared clad in their uniforms.

'We'll be late,' said the frog who was awaiting them, 'but we may as well make an effort: here's the car.'

The three entered the luxurious car which stood softly purring outside the palace door. The streets were already dark as they passed through them, and here and there they came across batallions of volunteers converging on Raymond Dock, from which the 3 ships had arranged to set sail.

'Here we are,' said Big. Suddenly stepping out, the 2 kings found themselves standing in the midst of a vast concourse of soldiers, drawn up as three sides of a square. On their right were lined up the Regular Mouselands, commanded by Colonel Pouter: opposite them were the volunteer additions to this regiment, under Corporal Puddiphat, who wore his tunic & sword as well as in other moments he did his morning-coat. On the left were the Chutneys, the largest force present, under command of the Colonel from whom they derived their name. In the background, the boys could make out the huge hull of the Indian Star, shillouetted against the star bespangled vault of heaven.

In the foreground was Fortescue, who came forward to greet them.

'Ah, Your Majesties, you've come nice and early: we can get our men on board at once.'

'Yes do,' said Big who wanted his dinner. 'Boys, you'd better make a speech to the men.'

'Yes, Yes,' said Fortescue.

'No,' said Hawki, 'they know already all the things that I should say.'

Big shrugged his shoulders, & Fortescue said 'Mouselands, right-turn! Embark.'

Their was a movement, a short march, & their place was bare.

'Mouselands Volunteers, right about turn! Embark.'

Puddiphat marched his men off into the night.

'Chutnies, left turn! Embark.'

They too dissappeared and the place was bare untill the spectators crowded over it. Big and Fortescue mounted the troopship, while the boys decended to their much smaller craft which they were going to navigate in person. A deep roar broke from the liner's horn, followed by a more modest blast from the *Thrush*, which lay beyond it, and after that the *Cygnet*'s shriller note.

The Little-Master, from the Indian Star's promenade deck noticed a widening gap between her and the wharf, & amidst ringing cheers the 3 ships dropped down the river.

CHAPTER XIV

The next morning, on coming on deck, the Little-Master found the vessel ploughing through a tumbled waste of grey water. Away to the port horizon (that is the south) he could make out the rocky islet of Rockphabel. Crossing to starboard, he saw the *Thrush* and the *Cygnet* forging ahead. The air was cool and bracing, and a fragrant odour of breakfast floating through the open door of the first class saloon filled the old frog with a feeling of healthy peace & comfort, rarely if ever obtained upon land.

'Upon my word,' he said to Quicksteppe who had just joined him, 'One could go anywhere in a boat like this. No need for those huge things they run on the "Ala" Line: this is just as comfortable and, I daresay, more sea-worthy.'

'Ah! You can have it very rough later on in this voyague.'

'Sure, what difference would that make to a boat like this?'

'Much. Anyway, let us come below & break our fast.'

Perhaps the meal was not as delicate a one as the Little-Master had imagined beforehand. Probably not. At any rate, when about an hour later he returned to the deck with a cigar, the glamour had gone from his surroundings. That evening the ship set her course due north, and confronted the series of huge billows which hurled themselves at her bow. The days were long since past when the *Indian Star* rose to a wave, & she now preferred to burrow through & let it fall thundering on her forecastle. She could still roll, however, as the Little-Master knew to his cost when his scalding soup at dinner was shot onto his tightly drawn dress trousers.

'Ah, upon my word,' cried the suffering frog, 'it was ridiculous to attempt the voyague in a cockle-shell like this.'

'Its a fine ship, Little-Master,' said Reginald Vant, who, being an old seamen, was acting as captain.

'And,' added Quicksteppe rather unfeelingly, 'you told us this morning that "One could go anywhere in a boat like this."'

'Ah no,' said Big, quite believing he spoke the truth, 'I never said anything of the kind. Excuse me a moment Fortescue.' With that he retired to change the boiling mass of clinging cloth which once had been dress trousers!

Next morning, the *Thrush* was steaming so close to the liner that one could shout from boat to boat. While Big was walking on the promenade of the *Indian Star*, Bar, the purser of the gunboat, inquired of some friend on board the troopship 'if the Little-Master made a habit of emptying his soup onto his knees?'

As that long second day of ups and downs wore on the Little-Master felt that not only had the glamour gone from sea life, but also that it had never possessed any. On board the *Cygnet* the boys were too occupied in the navigation of their vessel, in which they were assisted by only two men, to think of much else. On the gunboat *Thrush*, all was merry as usual. Bar rooked his mess-mates over their food & drink, & borrowed money from them with touching goodfellowship. For two or three days the *Cygnet* got seperated from the main expedition, and Big, who was by nature somewhat pessimistic, ordered the flags to be flown half-mast before they had been absent for 24 hours. However they returned on the third day, only having been driven out of their way by a violent tempest. After that Big insisted that the *Cygnet* should sail between her two fellow vessels.

On the 7th night out, to the Little-Master's unspeakable horror, the Chutneys got up an amateur performance of 'The Three Looneys'. And so, day after day, the little expedition sailed on northwards towards the Tracity Islands: sometimes they came in sight of the coast of Dolfin on their starboard, but they never touched for this continent was full of an army friendly to the Chess. After a sail of a fortnight, one morning when the steward came & called the Little-Master he also told him, 'We're in sight, m'lord.'

Big dressed very quickly and rushed on deck, very thankful that his not altogether pleasant voyague was over, and anxious to see the famous island of which he had thought for weeks.

CHAPTER XV

The sea was calm and of a pale grey color. The sky was cloudless and almost colorless, and countless gulls were wheeling overhead with loud and raucous screeches. The air was cold and still, and a feeling of excitement hung over the three vessels, for there, not five miles away was the largest of the Tracity islands.

The engines of the *Indian Star* had stopped when the Little-Master emerged from the saloon entrance, and paced briskly forr'ard to see the

Lord Big and General Quickstepge on board
the "Indian Star"

destination. Raising his field glasses to his eyes he could make out a rocky coast line some three miles long: and the tops of its beetling cliffs were surmounted by a continuous rampart through which sullen-looking guns peeped at intervals. On the top of the rampart he could descrie tiny figures, black against the sky.

Replacing the binoculars in their case, the Little-Master returned to breakfast and to the saloon.

'Well, Fortescue,' said he as he sat down, 'what's our programme for to day?'

'Well, Little-Master, you and their Majesties, I was thinking, would go to Von Quinklë & formally ask him to recapitulate: and on his refusal declare war.'

'Very well. I suppose we'll use the *Thrush*'s pinnace?'

'Yes. Steward, tell Captain Murray to bring his boat allong side & ask their Majesties to be ready after breakfast.'

'Yes, Sir.'

Half an hour later, the Little-Master was seated in the stern of the little steam pinnace and the boys in the bow. At a distance of 3 miles from the island they met a small motor boat, in which sat a pawn, who intimated to them the fact that they must enter his vessel and go blindfolded to the island, if they wished to see his Excellency.

'Boys,' said Big, 'this is a trap.'

However he submitted to having his eyes bandaged and taking a seat on the new vessel. For some time he could hear nothing but the hiss of the water as it curled round the boat's prow, but in about 10 minutes the singularly good hearing with which nature has endowed all frogs enabled him to perceive that they drew near some cliffs, and a few seconds later he guessed that the ship was passing through some narrow entrance: then the prow of the motor boat grated on something hard & they were told to step out. They were led for what the frog judged to be 200 yds, a door was opened, their bandages were whipt off and they stood blinking in the presence of His Excellency Frater Senior Von Quinklë.

They were in a small room with high ground-glass windows, and before them at a desk sat a mild-looking old man who somehow imppressed them. When he spoke his voice was mellow and so even that it was almost expressionless.

He said 'I adress, I believe, the Kings & Little-Master of Boxen?'

'You do,' said Lord Big.

'To what am I indebted for this pleasure?'

'We have come to demand that you cancel your trade regulation.'

'Pleasure before business! Try a little of this wine, it is '60 Middlehoff.' Big look at it doubtfully.

'Ah,' continued Von Quinklë, 'You think it is poisoned: don't apologise, quite natural.'

'Well,' said Big, 'get to business. Either you consent or you eat your words. Let me warn you resistance is useless.'

'I seem to have read that phraze somewhere before: its not original.'

'Sir, d— bother your impudence. Remember – '

'Whip me this insolent toad from the presence,' said the Chessman in the same even voice. Big's eyes were once more bandaged & he was hurried away, but the Frater Senior's injunctions were not literally carried out.

'Now,' he went on, 'have you two kings anything to say?'

'We declare war.'

'So do we.'

'Quite so. Good morning.'

Sometime later the pinnace came up under the counter of the Indian Star, and the news that war had been finally declared was joyfully received by all on board.

CHAPTER XVI

Next morning the *Thrush* slowly steamed round the island at a distance of 5 miles untill it was due north, so that the two larger boats were facing each other with the island between.

Captain Murray's orders had been to shell the island from the north, so that after nightfall the *Cygnet*, which was now lying beside the Indian Star, could creep up unobserved & make a night attack.

'Marines to the guns!'

Wilkins, the gunnery officer, and four marines quickly strode forr'ad to the armoured gun of the *Player* pattern stationed on the forcastle, for although the Captain had said with dignity 'to the guns', if truth be told the *Thrush* had only one gun! With them came Bar stripped to the waist, who on these occasions acted as powder-monkey, a menial but necessary office.

FIYING FROM H.M.S TRTUSK.

Murray slowly swung his vessel till she lay bow on towards the north rampart of the fortified island.

'Give it them,' said Wilkins as they came into position. One of the marines released a lever. There was a cloud of smoke, a deafening report and the *Thrush* rocked furiously from the shock. When the cloud cleared, they saw that the shell had merely dislodged a fragment of rock. At that moment a white patch appeared on the dark surface of the distant rampart, then a loud crash, and a shell skimmed the water a few feet off the gunboat.

So the exchange of shells continued all that long morning & afternoon. At about the fifth shell, one of Wilkins' gunners was picked off, and later the shock of one shell, which struck the hull, precipitated Bar into the cold green ocean. Fortunately he was soon picked up, having sustained nothing worse than a compulsory wash, of which Hogge, the mate, said he stood in great need. A couple of Castles were killed on the island, and a large stretch of rampart blown away.

However, the longest days must end, and at last the sun sank & darkness fell. The *Cygnet's* small deck was crammed with the scouting division of the 'Mouselands' under command of Colonel Pouter, and a portion of the 'Chutneys' under their own Colonel. The Rajah did not despise the menial position of engineer & Benjamin stationed himself at the wheel. In the little saloon sat Big, Fortescue, and Quicksteppe. As silently as possible Bunny brought his little boat under the cliffs & coasted along in search of a suitable landing place. But he could find no such thing, and in any case there was no opening in the high rampart on top. After a short consultation it was decided that as soon as any accesible point was reached, the quick-firing gun of the *Cygnet* should make a breach in the wall, & the men charge. For all but an hour the imperial rabbit drove his boat along the coast & had almost despaired when he came upon a steep sloping rock up which a man might with difficulty climb. Here he stopped, & turning his little gun towards the wall above him he fired it. There was flash, a loud report, and rumbling crash of stone work above as a portion of wall was hurled away. In an instant the men were scrambling up the bank with cries of 'The Chutneys!! The Mouselands.'

In a few minutes a grimy figure appeared from the engine room, which on closer inspection proved to be the rajah. He and Big and Bunny scrambled up the bank together; at the top they could make out clearly the form of the island, the whole centre of which was hollowed out by art or nature so as to form a lagoon or dock: opposite them was a narrow entrance to this lagoon between two huge beetling cliffs, through which they must have passed the foregoing morning. Over this was hung from a crane a huge cone of metal (point downwards) ready to drop on any unwelcome vessel. The whole island sloped down like a saucer to its central lagoon. In it was gathered a vast crowd of Chess of all sorts from the Pawn in his tunic & skullcap to the Bishop in his magnificent uniform. This crowd had been looking out northwards towards the Trush, but hearing the noise of Bunny's quick firer they turned & rushed towards the south. And in a minute Chess & Boxonians were fighting hand to hand.

CHAPTER XVII

The Boxonians rushed across the stone parapet and down the slope with the coarse grass brushing against their knees, and the Chess ran steadily upwards to meet them. But when the Boxonians were within a few paces of them they suddenly stopped short and presented to the mass of running men and animals an impenatrible wall of bayonets.

The Little-Master who had got up some considerable momentum on the downward rush only saved himself from being impaled on the bayonet of a certain sturdy Castle by leaping to one side with such suddenness that he was precipitated into the grass. The Rajah and old Quicksteppe kept close together in the centre of the press, while Bunny singled out for himself a white Pawn with whom he carried on a long and vigorous duel right down in the moist shingle on the edge of the lagoon.

As usually happens in a hand to hand engagement, the confusion soon became so inextricable that it was very difficult to make out what was happening. His Excellency, watching the melée from one of the beetling cliffs which surrounded the northern entrance, was in doubt what to do.

Suddenly those on the Southern side of the lagoon descried the bows of a boat slowly pushing their way through the entrance, all unconscious of the vast projectile suspended over their heads. Instantly from one of the guard-houses on the south a shaft of blinding illumination shot out flooding the curious scene with the white lustre of a searchlight. Big, in the midst of the fight, read on the vessel's bows the word 'Thrush'.

Turning he fled from the press, cutting his way through the struggling mass of Chess. At last he reached the stone parapet and ran at his full speed

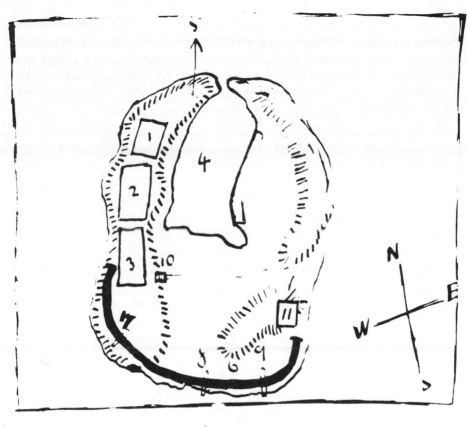

Scale :– Rosconian Miles.

1   2   3

MAP OF TRACITY ISLAND

KEY: –

1. Castles' Lodge
2. Pawns' Lodge
3. Knights' Lodge
4. Lagoon or Dock
5. Crane for Cone
6. Ramparts
7.

8. Guns
9.
10. Steps
11. Frater Senior's Lodge.

Max Length. – 6 miles
Max. Breadth. – $4\frac{2}{5}$ miles.

along it to the north. As he ran he could see a knight on the far side running in the same direction: Big realised what was going on. If this man reached the crane before he was within earshot of the *Thrush*, the projectile would be discharged and the gunboat irrevocably lost! On the two runners raced while below them the battle raged noisily and fiercely. Big had no thought for it now: his only aim was to warn captain Murray in time.

At last he judged that a shout would carry from where he was to the gunboat's bridge, and cried hoarsely 'Murray, steam ahead for all you're worth. Quickly.'

He heard the harsh clang of the vessel's telegraph and clouds of black smoke poured from her funnel: slowly at first but with ever-increasing velocity she stole forward, churning the waters of the narrow straight to fury with her screw: she was all out of the passage except the very stern where the saloon stood when the exhausted frog saw a figure appear running on the cliff-top high above his head: on and on the little figure came and it seemed that the *Thrush* was hardly moving.

Then the figure reached the massive crane and moved a lever!

Next instant there came a deafening crash of splintering wood, broken glass, and resounding iron. The stern of the *Thrush* was completely hidden from view by the columns of foaming water displaced by the huge cone, which rose to a great hieght and fell thundering on the stricken gunboat's deck. At the same moment the vessel's prow shot up till the armoured gun on her forcastle pointed at the pale moon above. For nearly half a minute she stood thus with her stern buried in the angry foam and her stem high and dry above it: then she gave a quiver and dropped to her normal level as quickly as she had risen from it.

She shot forward with more speed than she had known for many a day, staggered in her course, then listed over to port and lay quite still.

CHAPTER XVIII

Next morning when the grey dawn illumined Tracity island it displayed a curious scene. The Chess had retired into their fortified group of buildings on the West coast, leaving the Boxonians possessors of the rest of the island. The greater part of the expedition had however retired once more onto the Indian Star, leaving to hold the east half of the island the crew of the disabled gunboat.

Except for the small part of it held by the Chess the island was a gruesome-looking tract of bear grass covered with the ruins of the buildings destroyed by the shelling. Bar and his messmates, when left in charge, had wandered dismasily through the ruined streets littered with corpses and wrekage till they found a building of which only one wall had been blown off. It contained a sitting room, bedchamber, and entrance-hall.

'This,' said Bar, 'was Von Quinklë's own lodge.'

'Yes,' said Wilkins, 'I should think so. If so there ought to be some grub about.'

'What Ho!' said Murray from inside, 'Two bottles of rare old Middlehoff and a side of venison.'

'Come on!' cried Bar, 'light a fire.'

In an incredably short time the sailors were sitting contentedly round the brazier eating a hearty breakfast.

'I say, Captain,' said Bar with his mouth full of venison, 'what's the programme for to day?'

'They're bringing a couple of guns ashore and shelling the brutes out.'

'But,' said Hogge, the mate, 'is it true that the Little-Master's dead?'

'I dun'no.'

'Hullo,' said a voice they had almost forgotten. Turning round they saw a Chessknight of medium height, carelessly dressed, good natured and intellegant. It was Samuel Macgoullah! They all liked Macgoullah very much but this meeting was disagreeable. For after all he was a Chess: there was no getting away from the fact. He had lived in Boxen all his life, he spoke Boxonian, he thought Boxonian, and he drank 'Boxonian'. They had expected that he, like hundreds of other Chess, would ignore the war and keep away from it. It was foolish of him, they thought, to turn up now amidst those who were his friends in Boxen.

'Good morning,' said Murray awkwardly. Macgoullah laughed, 'You look as if you thought I'd got a bomb or something up me slieve! I've come with a letter to old Von Quinklë from Polly Green; I came last night in the *Bosphorous* and clambered ashore somehow.'

'Where did you get the letter?'

'One of Green's captains heard I was going up to Middlehoff with a cargo of lace (yes I'd payed the duty) and asked me to bring this along with me. He said that Green had given it him a week ago & he'd carried it about in his pocket all that time, forgettin' it. Ha! Ha! Just like a Greenite.'

Unexpected meeting of the crew of the "Thrush" with
Sml. Macgoullah (Master)

'I wonder ought we to confiscate the letter,' said Murray dubiously.

'Its all the same to me,' replied Macgoullah.

'Alright, I suppose you may as well take it on.'

Macgoullah set off at a brisk walk towards the fortifications, and, turning their eyes seawards the crew of the *Thrush* saw several boatloads of men and guns pulling for the shore.

The first one contained Their Majesties, Quicksteppe, and a small detachment of the Mouselands.

'I say, Murray,' cried the Rajah, leaping ashore hastily, 'Have you seen the Little-Master to day?'

'No, Your Majesty, I'm afraid not,' replied the captain. 'There was a rumour – '

'Yes?'

'That he was shot.'

'Goodness,' ejaculated Bunny, 'Doesn't anyone know?'

'Come, Majesties,' said Quicksteppe, 'it is no use questioning these gentlemen: we must go and search the island.'

'My Lord,' said Captain Murray, 'that is impossible: the whole island will be swept by the exchange of shells.'

'D—n your shells,' said Benjamin. 'I'm going to look for the Little-Master.'

'So am I,' said the Rajah.

'Your Majesties, Your Majesties,' pleaded Quicksteppe, 'it is unsafe.'

'Plug!' said the Rajah laconically, 'Are you coming?'

'If you are,' said Quicksteppe, and regardless of the expostulations of the sailors, the three set out for their ghastly search. Untill a shot was fired from the Chess citadel, it had been decided that the Boxonians should remain silent.

The two kings and the general were so intent upon their search that they did not stop to wonder why the guns of each side remained truculently silent. Their only thought was for the Little-Master. After walking wearily for nearly three miles of ruins and corpses they found themselves on the parapet where the frog had raced so furiously on the previous night. At the far end of it stood a half destroyed building.

Entering it, they glanced round. The floor, never of the best, had been shattered by a shell which had also in its flight pierced a huge hole in the roof. A damp unwholesome stench hung over the place and in one corner lay – the Little-Master.

CHAPTER XIX

For a minute the three stood in silence gazing at the huddled form. At last Bunny spoke. 'Is he dead?'

'I don't know.'

The Rajah advanced and touched the frog's shoulder. To his unspeakable relief the latter turned round, opened his eyes, and said irratably, 'Oh, there you are! Why didn't you look for me last night? I was here, and before I got back to the South of the island the boats had gone, and I could see no one about. Consequently I've had to pass the night here, which may prove a very serious thing for a frog of my age.'

'Thank goodness,' said Benjamin, 'we thought you were shot.'

'Ah, nonsense,' said Big, 'At any rate I want a meal.'

'Oh we can get that easily: the crew of the *Thrush* are breakfasting down there,' said Quicksteppe consolingly.

'Well come on boys.'

As the hungry Little-Master and his companions walked southwards, Bunny remarked, 'An awfully nice fellow that steward on the *Thrush* is.'

'Who's he?' inquired Big.

'Uh a fellow called Bar: a little hock-brown bear.'

'I *do* not like bears.'

'Not even the little hock-brown ones – ?'

'Ah they're the worst of the lot!'

'Why?'

'Ah they're impudent little creatures, and not only impudent but at times actually dishonest.'

'And what of the others.'

'Ah the grizlies are sour, cruel beasts, and the white bears are exasperating people.'

The boys and Quicksteppe were on the point of argueing the matter, when they were overtaken by a Chess pawn bearing a flag of truce and a sealed letter.

'Ah,' whispered Big, 'they are beginning to climb down.'

'For Your Lordship,' said the pawn handing Lord Big the letter.

It read as follows: –

> Sir:-
>
> We have just discovered
> that this war has been founded
> throughout on misaprehension
> Mr. Green posted to us a
> letter refusing our proffer-
> -ed monopoly: owing to
> Boxonian mismanagement
> this news did not reach us
> untill to day We therefore
> withdraw our decree.
>
> Signed ⵊⵊⵊ
> (Frater Senior)
> Tracit bh

A few hours later the war was formally declared at an end and on the following day preparations were begun for the return voyague. Von Quinklë, now thoroughly reconciled to the Boxonians, assisted in the mending of the *Thrush*, which in less than a fortnight was ready to face the return journey.

But although the war had passed off successfully, and with much less loss of life than could have been anticipated, Lord Big was very dissastisfied. He felt that somehow the whole affair seemed a mere burlesque, a play, since it was found that they had been fighting all this time for nothing. And the greater part of his troops shared this sentiment, and, on the whole, animosity against the Chess was increased rather than soothed by the sudden termination of the war. The news had of course to be telegraphed to Boxen, where the comic papers snatched it up and made the most of the episode.

CHAPTER XX

Nowhere in the world is fine weather so acceptible as in Piscia, the lovely island of which the Little-Master was a native.

Tousandpot, the chief town of the island was basking under a cloudless sky of that deep shade of spotless ultimarine so seldom seen in these latitudes. To the east lay acre upon acre of green fields rising in gentle slopes to where the purple mountain stood out against the sky-line. To the west was Tousandpot harbour, where the sparkling water reflected the color of the sky.

Alongside the jetty lay a small and immaculate fore and aft schooner, whose bows bore the legend 'Bosphorous': she was Macgoullah's boat. A few yards on was Polonius Green's latest venture, the *Puffin* a tidy tramp of just over 1000 tons register.

Out in the bay the *Thrush*, now fully repaired rode at anchor. The town was at this time being honoured by a visit from the boys and Court, of course accompanied by Little-Master Big.

PLAN OF TOUSANDPOT

KEY: –

1. The Tousandpot Arms Inn
2. Balcony
3. Railwaymens' House
4.
5. Detached Villas
6.
7.
8. Terminus of Piscian State Ry.Coy.
9. Perminant Way of Piscian State Ry. Coy.
10. Toadmore Station
11. Public Jetty
12. Putney's 'Palace' Music-Hall & Theatre
13. House of Parliament

14. Station Street
15. Shark Point Road
16. Kingryll Road
17. Toadmore Road
18. Common Storage Ground
19. Cliffs
20. Bathing Stage
21. Houses
22. Parliament Place

Population: – 300
Returning 2 members
Votes: – 123

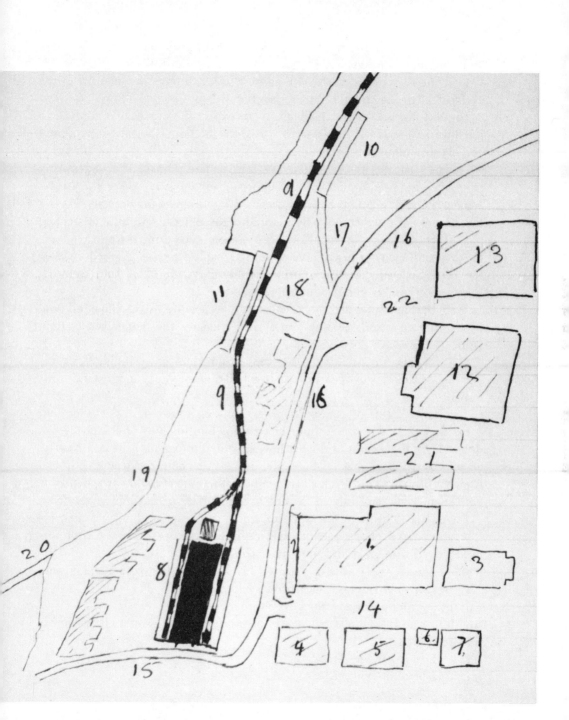

The latter was now strolling leisurely along the jetty, smoking a fine cigar and clutching a heavy walking stick. His heart was full of wrath, for Sir Goose, the barrister-detective, whom he had set to trace the offender of the golf-ball affair, had told him it was Jas. Bar.

Big had decided that it was hopeless to expect the purser of a gunboat to pay him £50, and his plan was now to sieze the bear when he came ashore and chastise him with his walkingcane.

At last patience was rewarded! An immaculate pinnace shot out swiftly from the side of the gunboat and approached the jetty where the Little-Master stood alternating between frenzied wrath and calm ferocity. At last the boat was brought under the jetty and the officers one by one stepped out. Murray, Hogge, Macphail, Wilkins, passed: next came the bear!

All unconscious of his coming doom the hapless purser climbed up onto the pier. Suddenly he was startled by hearing a voice exclaim near by, 'You're the bear! Don't deny it! Come here Sir!'

With that he was siezed by his collar and recieved a vicious blow followed by another an other. Holding him at arm's length, the frog talked to him, emphasizing each word with a cut.

'I – confess – I – don't – see – the – humour – of – stuffing – your – Little – Master's – bed – with – golf – balls. Do – you – understand – me – Sir!!!'

Bar had a habit of chattering when he was annoyed, and the present occasion was no exception: unfortunately for him his flow of eloquence was drowned by the torrent of the Little-Magisterial indignation. It is, I believe, an excepted axiom that all human things must come to an end: Bar had begun to despair of ever seeing his friends again, when at last the frog laid aside his walkingcane, and carried the chattering purser to the edge of the jetty.

Here, Big delivered a vicious kick upon the bear, at the same time releasing his hold on his victim's collar. The result was that the later was precipitated with great force into the harbour.

'You'd better stay where you are,' cried Big as Bar rose gasping, and shaking the water from his hock-brown muzzle.

Turning round, Big saw the boys approaching.

'Ah,' he said, 'I've just taught one of those bears a lesson he'll remember for a long time.'

'How?' inquired Hawki.

'I thrashed him with my cane,' said Lord Big.

Lord Big has occasion to corporally chast--ise Jas. Bar.

CHAPTER XXI

Since Polonius Green had quarreled with Viscount Puddiphat he had completely changed his mode of living. Morning coat suits, balls, and dinners had no longer any attraction for the parrot: in themselves they never had held it, but in the days when he was a friend of the Viscount's he had looked on them as the necessary steps to that vague yet enviable discomfort known as 'society'. But that was all over now: the fact that he had been bribed by Frater Senior Von Quinklë to get the Chess seats in the Clique of Boxen was now too universally well known to admit of any concealment, and this stamped out his chances of social success. For a week or so Polonius grieved over this and made one or two attempts to regain his lost status: they were all abortive. He had completely shut himself out by his action.

Finding restoration impossible, he gave up the idea and returned to the old life he had led before his tramp steamers had made him rich. Firstly he sold Shelling House to Sir Goose, who paid him half as much again as he had bought it for: he then built a small and homely house on the Murry docks. Finding a lot of cash on his hands he built himself two new tramps, the *Penguin*, and the *Puffin*, sister ships of one thousand and fifty tons each.

On the evening of the day which saw Bar soundly thrashed, Polonius Green was sitting smoking in the saloon of the latter vessel, which, as we have mentioned, was lying at Tousandpot.

Although the faint remnants of the lovely spring day poured in no feeble illumination through the open skylight and burnished portholes, the lamp was lit: in its yellow glare one could make out the outlines of [a] comfortable cabin. On either side was a bunk one for him and one for the mate. The floor was covered with a luxurious turkey carpet, for, although he had renounced society, Polonius had no intention of denying himself comforts which he could afford. In one corner was a large stove in which burnt a small fire, and on which sizzled a formidible kettle. On the walls, framed, hung Green's master's certificet, a calendar, and a badly painted oil-color drawing of the ship. On the far side of the table sat Willoughby, the mate, an able seaman who affected a great skill in matters sartorial.

The table, on which was a salmon & a tinned tongue, was laid for four.

Polonius was expecting company.

Small supper party on board
the 'Puffin'.

CHAPTER XXII

The door of the saloon was thrown open and two figures entered. The first was Mr Jas. Bar R.N., clad in an excellently cut chocolate-colored lounge suit, straw hat, and green and red waistcoat. He was followed by Samuel Macgoullah, dressed in his shoregoing blue serge suit and bowler hat.

'Good evenin', gents,' cried Green springing up. 'What on earth were you doing Bar, this afternoon?'

'When?'

'On the quay with the Little-Master.'

Bar colored with annoyance, which fortunately was invisible under his hock-brown hair.

[143]

'Oh,' he replied after a moment's hesitation, 'a little affair of honour, a little affair of honour!'

'Sit down,' said Green. 'I don't believe you Bar.'

'Of course not,' said Macgoullah, 'Come Bar, out with it!'

'Out with what?'

'The story of your thrashing.'

Bar gasped.

'Well, its all on your account Polonius.'

'Eh. Tryin' to kinder shift the responsability?'

'Well, if you hadn't been turned out of the Clique it would never have happened.'

'How so?'

'Butter please – If you hadn't come to me that night in the – (salt) – Schooner and persuaded me to stuff the Little-Master's bed with golf-balls, I would have been alright.'

'My dear little Bar,' cried Green, 'it was all your idea.'

'Yes, but at your instigation.'

'Anyway,' said Willoughby, 'the thrashing did him a world of good.'

Everyone except the bear himself heartily agreed with this statement.

'What do you think of the Little-Master?' inquired the Chessknight presently.

'He's a kod,' said Green.

'Perhaps,' said Bar, 'but he's alright about some things.'

'Fer instance – ' asked Green.

'Well he didn't make me pay for those golf balls. And although he insisted on engaging in a vulgar brawl on the docks, I'm not sure that paying wouldn't have been much worse.'

'Ah, but he's a friend of your's.'

'He is not,' said Bar with great emphasis. 'He hates all bears and especially the little hock-brown ones. Perhaps I might have become his friend by degrees, but by the golf-ball trick I locked the door to his acquaintance for good!'

THE END

'The Albatross'

THAN-KYU

A sketch

I

Lord Big was once a young frog. There was a time (before he was Little-Master) when he was small and even agile: when he sat on an obscure back bench in Parliament as an awe-struck fresh member: when he was taken but little notice of by the continent which he was destinned to rule – practically speaking: when his enemies could not annoy him worse than by calling him a 'callow tadpole'.

It was in *this* stage that he was when he fell dangerously ill and for many weeks lay between life & death. On his recovery he was sent on a short sea voyage to recuperate: his father, the old Big of Bigham, decided to send him to Than-Kyu, an obscure indepent state between Turkey and Pongee.

Accordingly he embarked on board the *Albatross*, a 500 ton trading schooner fitted with auxiliary paddle engines of 27 horse power (nominal).

The days of steering from amidships were as yet in their infancy, and the *Albatross* was controlled by a wheel on her lofty aftercastle. The captain was one Nicholas Redige, a stout puffin for whom Lord Big soon developed a great liking and admiration.

The Journey

The vessel was wooden-hulled, and the piston – at the top of its stroke – rose high above the deck through an oblong opening built for the purpose: the top of the boiler projected a couple of feet above the deck level, showing the dome and safety valves. With her hold full of coals she was making a tour to Constantinople calling at Than-Kyu. The saloon, which was situated in the aftercastle, and the cabins below it, could accomidate 12 passengers but Lord Big was on this occasion the only one.

Such, then was the vessel, on whose poop the young frog found himself, as she puffed and wheezed her laborious way out of Murry. Beside him stood Redige close to the wheel which was in the hands of a Chesspawn.

'Yes, m'lord,' said the skipper, 'its a fine life for them as likes it, and I dunno but that I wud not do it again. But I'll be d—d if I like these Turkish trips: give me a howling gale round tip if ye like, but nut a Turk.'

'Why?' asked the other.

'Wall,' said the puffin, 'ye can nut ever "have" them. And they're that slippery, m'lord, ye'd sooner hold a whiting. They'd never be stood at Herring's P'int.'

'I suppose not.'

'Its Than-Kyu ye'd be going fer, m'lord?'

'Yes. What sort of people are they?'

'The vairy worst. But some of them 'ill do fer a bit. But it's a gran' place.'

'I suppose so.'

'Aye, an' ye'll know it too! What was it the poet ses – "Danphabel with its thousand colored poplair-trees"? – But it ware'nt a sloop beside Than-Kyu.'

'"Colored copulas", I think.'

'Aye, that was it. But no matter, no matter – A p'int to port Joe – I never cud tell wan plant from another.'

'When will we make Than-Kyu?'

'Maybe in fur days.'

'Oh. Well you're calling there again on your way back – ?'

' – I am that.'

'Well you'll pick me up then. That'll be in about ten days – ?

' – Ten days? – What do ye take the old schooner fer? Ten – ? Why seven an nut an hour onder.'

'Oh, I apologise. She must be a fast boat.'

'Can't ye see fer yersel?' said Redige indicating the coast of Mouseland on their port side, which was moving very slowly past.

'Why, to be sure,' said Lord Big. 'And now I must bid you good night.'

'Right, m'lord. Shout for the stewaird, there's no bell.'

'Is that Than-Kyu?'

It was Lord Big who spoke. He and Redige were standing down in the belly of the ship hard by the top of the sizzling boiler: it was about four days after the conversation narated in our last chapter. As he spoke he pointed to a stretch of low-lying land far off on their starboard.

'That's it, m'lord,' answered the captain, 'as sure as I'm a puffing.'

'We'll be in, in about an hour?'

' – Three quarters, nut ever a minute more! But ye've a poor sort of opinion of my bo-at.'

'Not at all, but I know little about ships.'

'I have nut ever met anay one who knew less, begging yer pardon all the saime.'

'Oh, granted: I confess it myself. So you'll call for me in seven days?'

'Yes, m'lord.'

'Without fail?'

'I have nut ever failed a passengair,' said the puffin proudly.

Leaving the passenger to reflect on this he turned and ascended the steps to the aftercastle.

Lord Big walked forrad, and sat down on the lowest rung of the ladder which lead to the forecastle. The vessel was speeding along, with every stitch of canvas set, under the double forse of wind and steam: kealing over at a considerable angle with one of her paddle wheels buried in grey foam, and the other three quarters out of water, she was making a speed of nine knots per hour, no inconsidrable progress for the time of which we are speaking. Watching with eagerness the shoreline (which they were converging on with tolerable rapidity) he was able to make out the gleaming white domes and minarets of the town where he hoped to spend an enjoyable week. The minutes sped on broken only by the commands which Redige shouted occasionaly from the poop, and the hoarse reports of the lookout man.

At last, the schooner began to push her way into the commodius bight which the harbour of Than-Kyu was formed from. Bit by bit the skipper drew in his canvas, and the enginer stood ready to stop his machinary. At length she came alongside the stone parapet which was dignified by the

name of wharf: it was crowded with robed and bearded Islamites, who
mooved with cries and sloth. The gangway was shoved on board, and, lifting
his bag, Lord Big walked onto the soil of Than Kyu.

III

The pitiless glare of the sun beat down on the angular bazaar-street of the
wine-sellers, so brilliantly that it hurt Lord Big's eyes to look at the white
alabaster walls of the houses: that the clearly defined shadows appeared as
black as jet: a confused babel of shrill discordant voices filled the leaden
atmosphere.

Lord Big stood, bag in hand, looking around him. Half a dozen natives
surround him shouting to carry his bag. Giving it to one, he desired to be
shown to the 'Dragon' Inn. Following the man, he climbed street after
street ever upwards, untill, after quarter of hour's walking they halted before
a long low building. Entering he found himself in a low and ill-lighted
sitting room, furnished with three tables and some low benches.

His fellow-guests, three in number, were remarkable. One, a lama from
the north, sat in a dark corner swaying himself to and fro as he told his
beads: the second, a fat merchant of Constantinople, was eating some un-
savoury dish at the table: the third lay on the floor in the frog's path. He
was aged and fiery-looking.

'Would you mind moving, please Sir?' said Big.

The prostrate figure gave him a glance and shut his eyes again. The frog
reiterated his question, and this time it had no effect at all.

'Ah upon my word I wont stand it,' cried Lord Big, dealing the offender
a savage kick and proceeding indoors. The gaunt and bibulous figure rose
and cursed with a fluency and artistic finish that would have done credit to
a Clarendonian merchant captain.

So Lord Big continued to live at the Dragon Inn, as did also the other:
but the Frog forgot and he did not.

IV

On the seventh day, as Lord Big was walking happily along the road on
which the 'Dragon' was situated, he was surprised and somewhat alarmed
by the sudden and noisy advent of some half a dozen armed soldiers of the

governor: his dismay and wrath may well be imagined when the sturdy
rascals advanced to him, and, without leaving him time for expostulation or
query, gripped him firmly and proceeded to hurry him along at a brisk pace.

For a few minutes the unfortunate Piscian was too astounded to utter a
word, and when he had recovered enough to frame a sentence he found that
he had to devote all his breath and concentrate all his energy on the work
of running. His captors ran him through the labyrinth of steep thouroughfares which led to the harbour: on reaching it, the frog found two persons
who seemed to expect the arrival of his jailors and himself: one was the
excellent gentleman who he had kicked on his first day, and his companion
was His Excellency the Imperial Deputy Governor for Than-Kyu. The
latter spoke 'My good Sir, I have a disagreeable duty to perform: it is the
Emperor's law that no foreigner should stay on our soil for six consecutive
days: you have outstayed your time, and must therefore be thrown out.'

'Thrown out? Come Sir, this is irregular,' cried the frog, 'and whats more I won't stand it. I knew nothing of this law.'

'You should have made it your business to learn our laws,' said the gentleman Lord Big had kicked.

'Oh its you I have to thank for this?' said Big.

The gentleman bowed.

At a monosyllable from the governor the frog was born to the jetty's edge. Then he felt a sudden thrill, a rush of air, and the smack of luke-warm water.

Ten minutes later a dripping frog stood disconscolately on the deck of the Albatross. 'Well Redige,' it said, 'I can't go back there for some time.'

'Nut ever,' said the puffin.

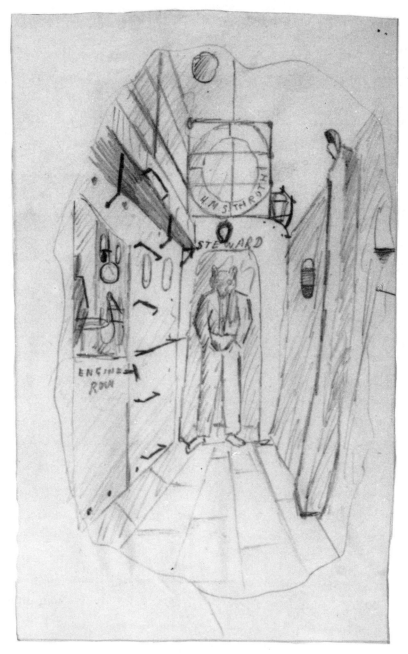

James Bar on board H.M.S. *Thrush*

THE SAILOR
A Study

VOLUME I

CHAPTER I
THE TRAVELLER

The Charlestown express panted its noisy way into the Murry terminus, and its entrance was the signal for a rush of eager porters towards the edge of the brown platform whose surface afforded landing to the passengers of the train. As the brakes squeaked and the wheels ceased to revolve, the door of a first class compartment opened to give egress to a passenger, of whom it is desirable for us to take a brief survey.

He was a strong & wiry young cat, whose shortness of stature was no deformity, since the rest of his well-moulded figure was modelled in harmony with his inches. His face had nothing in common with most of his fellow-countrymen, that soft expression of languid sloth, which is so often predominant in a cat's physiognomy, being replaced by one of an intellectual briskness whose vigor amounted almost to ferocity. His head, like that of all cats, was handsome and well placed on his firm shoulders, and was adorned with a wealth of soft grey fur which betrayed him to be a so-called 'Persian'. His firm, elastic step, his clear and inquisitive expression, the decision and composure with which he responded to any remark of his fellow-travellers, all tended to show a character bubbling over with youthful enthusiasm and decision. Although his attire betrayed no foppery, nor even an undue attention to the toilet, his blue serge suit and carefully knotted brown necktie were neat and well kept.

Having collected his belongings from the van, and, not without difficulty procured a cab, he directed the driver to the Royal Wharf, a well-known centre of the Murry docks. As he was driven through the busy streets of

[153]

the capital of Animalland, the young, home-bred cat, could not help being interested by the curious and vivacious panorama which they presented to his view. The tall buildings, and the crowded thouroughfares, could scarce fail to impress one who had seen only the quiet avenues of Charlestown, or the sleepy markets of feline villages.

Thus agreeably occupied in watching surroundings as novel as they were attractive the young cat did not observe the lapse of time or the distance his vehicle travelled, and was somewhat startled on percieving he had halted, and his driver had opened the door to admit the grey wet fog and thin rain which were at present honouring the metropolis by their presence.

'Oh – er – yes: where do I want to go? Oh, do you know where I could get a waterman to row me out to His Majesties ship *Greyhound*?'

'Aye, Sir. Would ye be wantin' the pinnace, like?'

'If I can have her,' rejoined the cat. By way of answer, the cab driver siezed on his fare's solitary trunk and bidding the latter follow, bore it to the edge of the wharf, and, peering down into the fog, cried 'Mr Mus?'

The traveller's keen eyes had not much difficulty in deciphering a small steam pinnace lying in the oily water below his feet. In the stern, what had before resembled an inanimate bundle, but which was now presumably 'Mr Mus', rose and shouted up in a strong mouse accent, 'Is thon you, Harvey?'

'Aye. A've got the gent here.'

'A'll just bring me wee boat to the steps, and you have peace.'

In case our readers have not guessed it, it may be expedient to state that our young feline was a naval marine officer, who, having been just recently freed from the trammels of a naval college, was on his way to join his first vessel. Thus, as may be readily understood, he listened with mingled emotions of expectancy and nervousness to this dialogue, and gazed into the steaming mist, in a vain attempt to make out the vessel which was already in his mind the scene of many triumphs and adventures. But the driver of the pinnace did not allow him much time for such reflections, and, pulling his vessel up to a flight of steps built for that purpose against the towering wall of the wharf, cut them short by a respectful but cherry 'Hop aboard, Sir! You're Mr Cottle, the new marine-officer, are'nt you?'

'Yes,' returned the youth, 'and I am speaking to – ?'

'Jerry Mus, Sir, second engineer and head of the foc 'sle.'

Greatly relieved to find that he was as yet in the presence of his official inferior, Alexander Cottle paid the cab-driver, and ensconced himself in the stern sheets of the pinnace, where a couple of padded seats were provided for the engineer and his passenger. His trunk was settled on a corresponding seat in the bow, the mouse opened his throttle, and the young feline set off towards the *Greyhound* and towards his naval career.

As the little boat puffed noisily across the oily waters of the river, he had plenty of time to observe his companion and guess at his probable position on board the ship. Mus was a short, spare mouse whose lean and ragged muzzle savoured more of the rat than of that tribe to which he professed membership.

After some ten minutes run, a black mass loomed up in the mist, and Cottle's heart beat strong as he gazed at last on the vessel which he had so often constructed in his mind, and saved from disaster in his dreams. She was a second class cruiser, and had been built but a week ago, so that even through the curling fog she looked bright and new. Of her details, Cottle could make out little, and so, without any knowledge of what was before him, he stepped on board.

CHAPTER II
THE SERVICE

It was not untill Cottle had gained a point of vantage by coming up to the deck of the cruiser that he realized that she was not lying alone in the river but was alongside a small gunboat from which numbers of men – the whole crew it seemed to him – were engaged in transporting all sorts of goods from rifles and canon to tables and dishes. So engrossed were these persons in their task that the young cat was able to stand unobserved for some time, and contemplate the busy scene, which was so unlike any former experience of his. He conjectured, and rightly so, that the smaller vessel was the gunboat *Thrush*, which was now being put out of commission, while her officers and crew were taking over the newly-built *Greyhound*.

On the navigating bridge stood a tall, cleanshaven man, whose handsome but somewhat caustic face was overcast by an expression of worrey and anxiety. This person, Cottle put down in his mind as Commodore Murray, the master of the vessel, in which surmise he was correct. A young and intellegent cat, who knew by sight the uniform of each rank and department, had naturally no difficulty in mentally fixing the majority of the officials who were engaged in transporting the goods.

1. Bathroom.
2. Officer's cabins.
3. Engine-room.
4. Gangway to Safety Valve.
5. Starboard Boiler
6. Boiler Room.
7. Coal Bunker

8. Coal Shoot.
9. Wireless operator's room.
10. Forecastle
11. General Store.
12. Lobby
13. Lock-up.
14. Condenser

15. Officers' Stove.
16. Shaft Room
17. " Tunnel.
18. Gun (Maxim)
19. Anchor Winch.
20. Hatch-way
21. Foremast.
22. Wheel Navigation Room

H.M.S. "GREYHOUND"

2nd class cruiser.
Home Squadron
4321 Tons.
Blt 1912. Gov. Yrd
Colombo. Ceylon.
Triple Expansion
Twin Screw.
Max. Speed - 19. knots

22.
23.
25
21.
18
20
19
8
9
12
10
11
7
35

er do.   31 Mainmast.
ha stacks.   32 Rudder
ines Mess.   33 Starboard Screw.
? by   34 Gig.
marters office 35 Ram.
er's mess.   36 Quick Firing
nter Deck   Guns.
dge Deck

By the saloon door stood a short bear, so short indeed that even Cottle might look over his head. He was plump and well nourished, not to say bloated, and his fur which was of the richest hock-brown color was fastidiously combed and brushed back over his little bullet head: he wore a broad, all-embracing smile, and looked absurdly satisfied with himself and all the world. He was clad in dusty blue trousers and a long makintosh. This grotesque personage, however, seemed to exercise unlimited authority over his fellows, and from his post shouted tyranical orders to those who were at work. Thus in spite of a certain absence of decorum in his attire and an insignificance of countenance and stature, Cottle could not help thinking that the little bear was an inspecting admiral at the least.

As he was reflecting in this strain he felt a light touch on his arm, and, turning round, found himself face to face with the individual whom he had espied a few minutes ago on the navigating bridge.

'Ah!' said the stranger, 'I suppose you are Mr Cottle, the junior marine officer?'

'Yes,' replied the other, 'I – '

'Well, may I ask,' interrupted the Commodore, 'what you intended to do or how long you purposed to stand here and watch the view?'

'Really Sir,' replied Cottle, covered with embarrassment at such a question, 'Really, I didn't quite know what to do.'

'You ought,' said Murray, 'to have come and reported yourself to me as soon as you came aboard, and I'd have given you a job. But there's plenty of work, still to be done. You see that big man with the moustach over there? That's Mr Wilkins, the gunnery-officer, your chief. Go and get a job from him.'

With these words the stranger hurried off, leaving the newcomer in a somewhat breathless condition. Cottle feared he had not made such an impression on his new master as he should have liked, and hastened to make amends by hurrying towards Mr Wilkins, who was a very big, loosely built man, with a lazy, good-natured face, and curling chestnut hair and moustaches: he stood sprawling against the wall of the central deckhouse, and blinked recognition as the cat approached.

'So you're our young friend Alexander Cottle, are you?' he said, 'and you want a job? No accounting for tastes!'

Cottle made an affirmative noise.

'Well,' continued his Mentor, 'the best you can do is to go into the armoury & see that the fellows put things straight: I've got to see them out of the *Thrush*. Dear old *Thrush*! Do you remember – but that's an old yarn. Be off!'

Cottle scurried through the deckhouse door, and, having accosted the first marine he met as to the whereabouts of the armoury, descended thither and passed the rest of the morning working harder, perhaps, than anyone on board. It was, therefore, with relief, that he heard the bell for lunch, and rushed on deck to find his new friend, Wilkins. The latter was on the promenade and escorted him to the saloon: on their way, Cottle enquired 'Who's that hock-brown bear, who's managing everything? Some admiral?'

The other laughed uproarously, and said 'Why, its only little James Bar, the steward.'

'Who called me steward?' cried the bear himself, appearing from the saloon: turning to Cottle, he said in a highly patronising tone, 'I, my little friend, am second lieutenant, James Bar, R.N., paymaster and head of the victualling department. You mustn't believe all Wilkins tells you.'

Whether it was the condescension of the little bear, or Cottle's own pride is uncertain, but this speech left a highly disagreeable impression on the cat's mind. As he was trying to choke down what he considered to be a mere prejudice they arrived at the saloon and sat down to a well deserved luncheon. Cottle noticed one new face in the officer's mess, and he was formally introduced to its owner as Macphail, the engineer. He was a spare, sour but not unkindly man, whose demeanour, which was grave and even morose, seemed to point to a greater age than that attained by any other members of the mess, save only the Commodore.

The conversation during the meal turned upon naval topics where the young cat had little to say. Just as they were rising from the table, a sailor entered to say that a message had just come from Oliver Vant, the first Lord, that Mr Cottle was to go ashore to the admiralty at once.

CHAPTER III
THE POLITICIANS

Although the city of Murry actually stands on Animallandish ground and is separated by water from any part of India, yet it is here, to their stately palace of Riverside that the monarchs of these two united nations chiefly resort. And here too the Little-Master follows them. The Little-Magisterial office is, as everyone knows, a weighty and responsible post, but bearing this in mind we may still say that Lord Big filled it admirably.

This remarkable frog, in addition to his many excellent qualities, posessed an advantage over his two sovereigns which was of great utility to himself. As a youthful frog he had been their tutor, and for several years discharged the duties of that post well and devotedly: and since princes of the blood royal have extremely little chance of associating with their own fathers, the two princes had come to regard Lord Big, if not as a parent, at least as an esteemed and venerable relation. Hence in his capacity of Little-Master (which, I may add for the benefit of foreigners, is an office comprising the duties of Speaker of the Double House and adviser general of the Kings), in this capacity, I say, he exercised a power, which, if he occasionally misdirected it, he at any rate always meant for the best.

Such was the worthy who was anxiously pacing the Grand Gallery of Riverside Palace, with an anxious and impatient expression on his handsome face. He was clad in a sombre suit of serge, well cut in the fashion of some ten years ago, and again and again turned his great amber eyes to the clock, as if he awaited a guest. As the devoted piece of mechanism startled its master by booming three oclock just by the Little-Magisterial ear, the door of the gallery was opened, and a footman announced 'Lord Oliver Vant, and Field-Marshall Fortescue, to see his Worship.'

These two individuals entered and advanced towards the frog. The former, of whom we have already heard as First Lord of the admiralty, was a tall, gaunt pig, of exceedingly melancholy but kind countenance. He was clad in the braided morning-coat & silk-stockings pertaining to his office, and walked with his tiny eyes fixed on the stone pavement before him. His companion was a man of medium hight, plainly clad in a sober suit. His face was all alive with vigour and interest and his eyes had a piercing glance that seemed to be ubiquitous. These two persons, respectively the heads of the naval and military war-offices, were men of widely different characters.

Why the former had attained to his post, was a mystery which few Boxonians could solve: he was a pompous and highly unpractical philosopher, on whom the veriest simpleton could impose with ease: by trace, he was originally a stockbroker, and in this profession he displayed an intelligence quite out of keeping with his usual character.

Fortescue, on the other hand, was a brisk, practical soldier, who had made an attempt so vigorous to reform the army, that he was now one of the least popular men in Boxen.

Such then were the frog's visitors, and glad he seemed to see them.

'Well?' he said.

'My dear Little-Master,' said the pig, 'It is as we feared. On consulting our friend Putney, the treasurer, he confirms your opinion that the National debt is so large that Boxen may scarcely keep her head above water, let alone see to reforming the services.'

'And,' put in Fortescue, 'in their present condition they are quite unfit to defend the country against any first rate power.'

'Well,' said Lord Big, 'where lies the fault? What exactly is wrong in them? How can it be mended?'

'By money!' snapped the Field-Marshall.

'And not only by money, my young friend,' said Oliver, 'but by reform. It is not the lack of ships or armament that has degenerated our navy into what it is. It is the incompetency and immorality of individuals – the lack of "esprit de corps".'

'Ah such nonsense,' said the Little-Master, forgetting all conventions, 'Sure, you may talk all night like that and never strike anything concrete.'

'And yet, My Lord,' said Fortescue, 'There is truth in Lord Vant's remarks. The officers set a bad example.'

'Oh, they do?' said Lord Big, 'Well drum them all out.'

'One cannot,' said Fortescue, 'act like that in this case. It is a tone we move against, not a concrete offence.'

'Or rather,' observed Oliver, 'an absence of tone.'

'Well,' said Big, 'I confess I don't know what to do!'

'Listen!' said Oliver, 'There is a steady stream of young recruits issueing all the time from our naval and military colleges, and in them we must place our hope. The present generation is too far gone to be influenced by any efforts of ours. It is our duty, therefore, to choose out a trustworthy young fellow in each ship or regiment and make it his work to reform that ship or regiment. If he is young, enthusiastic and discreet, and is well-warned against those with whom he must contend, he has every hope of success.'

'Your scheme is excellent in theory, My Lord,' replied the Field-Marshall, 'but, I fear, impracticable. Where shall we find such young officers, and how will we ensure their worth?'

'The scheme's all right,' said Lord Big, with great approval in his voice.

Riverside Palace, Murry

'Well,' said Vant, with the air of a conjurer who has just found the egg, 'I have, providentially, brought with me, for experiment, a young man whom I have watched carefully through his college career, and of whose integrity and patriotism I am convinced. Allow me to bring him from the ante-room.'

'By all means,' replied the Little-Master, with interest.

CHAPTER IV
THE MISSION

Lord Oliver Vant left the gallery and returned a few moments later, leading with him a young feline naval officer, who, as my readers have doubtless guessed was none other than Alexander Cottle, who was naturally both surprised and embarassed at being thus ushered into the presence of the virtual ruler of Boxen.

'This is my young friend,' said Vant with an air of proprietorship, 'and, I trust, a fine precursor to the line of reformers whom we hope to send out.'

'What is your name?' enquired Lord Big.

'Alexander Cottle, My Lord,' returned the cat.

'And are you aware of the purpose,' asked Fortescue, 'for which Lord Vant brought [you] here?'

'I know, My Lord,' replied Cottle, 'that his Lordship intends to reform the navy: but I have not yet been informed what part I may endeavour to play in such a work.'

'Well,' said Oliver, 'you entered to day on your first ship, and you as yet know little of your fellow-officers. You are young, and, I trust, vigorous, and I am entrusting you with a task which may alter the world.'

Cottle glanced at his muscular shoulders, as if expecting to see them crushed by such an imposition. Oliver continued, 'Will you endeavour by every means in your power to reform and cleanse your ship? You will have opposition, and you will find it uphill work. But success is not impossible. One word of warning' – he whispered these words in a voice inaudible to the rest of the company – 'on your ship you will find a mischievous little bear: his case is not hopeless, you may reform him.'

'I will try, My Lord,' said Cottle, 'but I am not quite clear as to what I must reform.'

'The tone,' said Lord Big.

'But, My Lord,' said the young cat, 'I can't see anything wrong with the tone.'

'Such nonsense!' said Lord Big hotly, 'If you –'

'Remember,' said Oliver, 'the boy has not been on this ship for twenty-four hours.'

'Well,' put in Fortescue, 'has Mr Cottle our leave to quit the palace?'

This was replied to in the affirmative, and Cottle walked out of Riverside as one in a dream. On his way to the palace, Lord Vant had delivered to him a long diatribe on the decadence of the navy, to which the former had listened at first with incredulity & afterwards with deep sorrow. The idea that the good pig might [be] exagarating or mistaken never occured to Cottle, who saw the ideal navy, which he had pictured in his mind, fall to pieces like a castle of cards. Against Bar, I am sorry to say, he was only too ready to believe ill, for the lax, humorous and somewhat loose character of the bumptious little bear could not but clash with the enthusiastic and strong ways of the cat. But it was a cruel blow to him to think of his new friend Wilkins as a criminal, for, after Vant's declamation, he regarded him as little better. This then was the navy!

But he swelled with pride as he thought of the mission which he had undertaken, and in imagination saw himself already famous as the Remaker of Boxen's Navy. It never struck the young patriot that there was anything ludicrous in the idea of his, a young lieutenant, being entrusted with the reformation of such sailors as Murray or Macphail.

Thinking thus, he took an electric tram through the lighted streets to the Royal Wharf, where, as the pinnace was drawn up beside the mass of lights which showed the *Greyhound*, he payed a waterman to row him out.

As he entered the saloon, whence a glow of warm, red light proceeded, he saw a figure advancing to meet him. It was Bar.

'Hullo', said the paymaster with a laugh. 'What have you been doing with the admiralty? I know Vant a bit myself. What did you think of him?'

'I saw,' replied Cottle stiffly, 'nothing to object to in the character of his Lordship.'

'Well,' said Bar angrily, 'you needn't talk like that about it.'

Cottle saw Wilkins in the oblong of light cast by the open saloon door, &, brushing past the truculent little hock-brown [bear] was greeted by the gunnery officer's cheery 'Hullo, Cottle, you're too late for shore-leave, that is if you want any dinner. The pinnace is just going.'

So Cottle ate his meal alone, and went to bed, meditating on the strange happenings of his first day of naval life.

CHAPTER V
THE PAYMASTER

The first person to awake next morning on board the *Greyhound*, or at any rate among the officers, was our little friend Jas. Bar. This worthy, despite the carouse in which he had indulged overnight, awoke with a clear head, ready to face whatever the day might bring.

As he lay in his bunk, he realized that with his transportation to his new vessel a new stage of life had begun for him and his comrades: he saw, with gloomy foreboding, the timetable on his wall which callously ordered twice as much work a day as he had done on board the *Thrush*: and, worst of all, he thought of his new mess mate, Alexander Cottle. Conceit and indulgence had not blinded the little bear so much that he could fail to realize that the newcomer would prove a very important factor in the internal economy of the ship, and, being a shrewd judge of men, he guessed that the cat would be not only vigorous himself but also eager to impart this quality to those about him.

Then again there was that visit of Cottle's to Vant! Bar himself was in the highly embarassing position of being one of the admiral's "protégés", and, although he by no means enjoyed this state of things, he had no desire to share it with a youngster whom he saw would be his rival.

With such thoughts as these in his mind the paymaster arose, and, dressing himself in a threadbare working uniform, lit a cigarette and went on deck. As the bear was slowly pacing the promenade, and viewing the buildings which lined either side of the river, he was met by Cottle, who, clad in nothing but his native fur, stood dripping with salt water.

As Bar had no intention of letting his feelings be seen, he said cheerily, 'Fallen overboard, Cottle?'

'No.'

'What's been happening then?'

'I had a bathe.'

'What??'

'I had a bathe.'

'Where?'

'In the river.'

One could have knocked Bar down with a feather.

'Do – you – mean – to tell me – you went overboard – into the water – on purpose?'

'Certainly.'

Bar stood with a gaping jaw for a few seconds and then burst into a laugh. Then he began again in a confidential tone.

'By the bye, Cottle, what had Vant got to say to you yesterday?'

'Oh,' said the other evasively, 'he just talked about the navy.'

'Yes, but what did he say?'

'That, Mr Bar, is [a] matter which concerns myself alone.'

'Oh come now! Just as a friend.'

'Really, Sir, our extremely slight friendship does not seem to justify my abusing the confidence which Lord Vant has reposed in me.'

'Oh!' said Bar, unable to keep up his friendly manner any longer, 'Well one of these days, let me warn you, the whole mess will feel justified in abusing your ears.'

Further friction was fortunately cut short at this period by the clanging of the breakfast bell, and a quarrel which might have proved serious, was added by each opponent to an already bulky series of grudges, to be paid at some future date. Perhaps it would have been better had they ended it there!

That morning a late member of the mess arived in the person of Hogge, the first lieutenant. This worthy was a hardy pig, who, although by no means such a scapegrace as Bar, was yet the leader of the crew in all desperate enterprises, and a skilful mediator between them and their caustic commodore. Of Cottle he took hardly any notice, and displayed no interest when the paymaster privately explained his quarrels with the newcomer, answering to such narratives, 'That he saw no reason for interfering in Bar's matters, and was content to oppose Cottle when he encountered him.' Thus the diplomatic lieutenant secured his popularity with all parties, and made a sturdy effort to keep these feuds from Murray's knowledge.

Cottle's second morning was employed in getting the *Greyhound* ready for her departure which was to take place on the 8 oclock tide on the next day. The bear was kept busily employed in making up an inventry in his office, while the cat was occupied in another part of the ship superintending the stowage of amunition. The voyague which the vessel was to undertake was that of bearing sealed dispatches to the flagship of the Clarendonian fleet – a task, which, in the present season of winter, could not be accomplished in less than six weeks.

That afternoon as James Bar was enjoying a few minutes well earned rest on the quarter deck he descried a very neat pinnace putting off from the wharf towards the *Greyhound*, which, when it had come alongside, proved to contain no less a personage than his own particular patron, Lord Oliver Vant. As soon as the good admiral had discharged his business with the commodore & was preparing to go, he was accosted by the head of the victualling department and led into the little box full of blotting paper & calendars which the latter termed his office.

'Well,' said the first Lord when he was seated, 'and what is your grievance, my little bear?'

'Look at this, M'Lord!' said Bar, holding out the new timetable.

'Well, I see an ordinary timetable.'

'Ordinary!' piped the bear, 'I have at least three hours office work every day, besides my duties as social head of the vessel.'

Vant regarded his protege over his spectacles and said, 'But, my good little bear, you must have something to keep you out of mischief.'

Thus admonished gravely, as if he had been a child of five, the poor paymaster could but say, 'that it would wear him out', and wrung the pig's hand affectionately ere he embarked upon such a fatal cruise.

That night Cottle took advantage of the shore leave to go and visit a friend in the town, while his messmates hurried off to a music-hall. When, at least, he flung himself on his bunk, he could not help lying awake to think, not only of the events of the day, but also of his coming departure on a voyague which was full of improbable horrors and still less probable successes.

CHAPTER VI
THALASSA!

Cottle was awake and up betimes on the morning of [his] first voyague, anxious not to lose a moment of the scene of departure. When he came on deck, he found no one there save a couple of marines who were busily engaged in hosing the boards untill they were as white as driven snow. The fog and mist had happily cleared off, and been replaced by a cold, clear sky and a stinging west wind, which, even in the seclusion of the river, stirred up curling riples and told of roaring seas outside. No sooner had the huge clock posted above the Double Parliament boomed the two strokes announcing half past seven than there was stamping of feet on the ladders and a crowd of men and animals, some of them hardly awake, tumbled up and stood as if expecting some theatrical pageant: nor were the officers any different in their habits, for Cottle observed his messmates standing on the promenades in a thick little group and gazing up at the navigating bridge. Just as the novice was about to enquire from his friend Wilkins the meaning of this pantomime, Murray appeared from the saloon entrance and took up his position on the bridge.

'As you know,' said the Commodore, 'we are to go, this voyague, to the Clarendonian waters, and judging by the wind in here, it will be no child's play either. Before we start, I should like to recomend some of our number, who have plenty of time to spare' – here he looked hard at Mr Bar – 'not to occupy it in turning my ship into a pandemonium: no tricks, this trip, paymaster. With this sixpence I will, as usual, toss for choice of first watch. Call Mr Hogge!'

'Heads!' said the pig.

'Heads it is.'

'We'll stand the first,' said Hogge.

'My watch below! Good morning, Mr Hogge.'

With these words the worthy commodore turned and left his bridge. While wending his way saloon-wards he caught sight of Cottle, standing leaning on the bulwarks and gazing round with interest.

'Now then, Cottle, what are you doing? Did you grow there?'

'No Sir. I don't know which watch I am in.'

'Well, why didn't you ask me before? Eh? Well you stand Hogge's watch. Look sharp to the bridge!'

Cottle suited the action to the word and hastened up to the bridge deck, and onto the bridge, a sacred spot where as yet he had not ventured. It was at present occupied by two persons, Hogge, standing at the port end, and a sailor stationed at the wheel. Hogge turned as he heard the hurried step of the cat.

'Oh you have turned up? Do you know what to do?'

'Not exactly.'

'Well, you take the starboard side of the bridge, and when ever we pass a boat take its name and owner and tonnage and carry them aft to the ears of your friend Mr Bar, for him to enter in his log.'

Hogge shot a shrewd glance at his companion to see what effect his mention of Bar would have, and in so doing saw the cat endeavouring feverishly to take the names of the countless vessels which plied to and fro in the great river.

'Of course,' said the pig with a chuckle, 'you needn't report any ship till we get into the open.'

With a fervent sigh of relief the young cat abandoned his Herculean task, and was able to view calmly the progress of the vessel through the widening Jemima. When once Hogge had telegraphed to Mus to put his engines at full speed it did not take the brand new cruiser more than twenty minutes to reach the town of Topsy, which stands at the mouth, and turn round northwards in the open sea. Then first did Cottle realize what small riples in the river may betoken considerable billows out at sea. The great grey masses of water struck the *Greyhound* repeatedly on her port quarter so vigorously that she reeled and heaved, rendering it no easy task for Cottle to maintain his station.

Meanwhile our ursine friend had not been idle. As the commodore walked into the saloon after delivering his homily, he was met by Bar, who had, with his usual audacity, determined to find out his master's views on Alexander Cottle. The little bear was, of course, too old a hand to rush headlong at such a delicate job, and had prepared a long conversation with which to cover his curiosity and to sound the commodore.

'Well,' said he cheerfully. 'Its a nice morning we've got for starting.'

'Yes,' returned the other looking at his paymaster suspiciously.

'I see,' went on Bar, 'you had bad luck with the toss: or do you like to stand the other watch?'

'Yes, I think I do,' said Murray, seeing that Bar was bent on talk.

'By the way,' asked the latter, 'which watch is Cottle in?'

'Hogge's.'

'Humph! I thought I saw him standing on the promenade, after Hogge had taken the bridge.'

'Yes: he didn't know which watch he was in.'

'Didn't he ask you before?'

'No. He's that sort of chap.'

This was more hopeful.

'What sort of chap?'

'Oh, quiet and moony.'

Bar had now got what he wanted, and he went to pace the quarterdeck in happiness. Which happiness, however, might have not been so alloyed had he been aware that Murray had scented Bar's plan and returned a verdict about Cottle, which he was far from thinking.

CHAPTER VII
THE QUICK-FIRERS

The watches in the Boxonian navy are from 9 to 3 & 3 to 9, so that the young cat, having come off the bridge at 3 in the afternoon, returned to his post at nine. The darkness had been thick since four, and when he stepped out of the saloon the *Greyhound* was plunging heavily forward in the snowy breakers which sent a shower of stinging spray as far as the bridge, as her bow buried itself in their jet black mass. Mindful of his delinquencies of that morning, Cottle had allowed himself plenty of time, and, when he arrived on the bridge deck, the other watch were still at their posts. The cat, who had never till now experienced any more terrible sea than that which he might have encountered in his passage from Boot-town to Bombay, had no small ado to stand upright on the slippery, tossing bridge deck. Presently a red point of light appeared from below, which proved to be Hogge's cigarette, and at the same time a hammering of feet for'ad told that the lieutenant's watch were ready. With a muttered greeting to Cottle, the experienced pig mounted the bridge, accompanied by the former and a steersman.

'Good night, Hogge,' said Murray, as he turned to go below. 'We'll have dirty weather before you've picked up the Salting.'

'Yes,' said the other gravely. 'Good night.'

To Cottle it had seemed bad enough on the bridge deck, but on the narrow, unprotected gallery of the bridge, his sensations were indescribable. All, of course, was as black as pitch, save for the red glimmer of the binnacles and the faint glow of the port & starboard lights: the vessel's bows were marked only by the phospherescent ridge of foam, and the intervening forecastle was a velvet void: and the whole was observed from a narrow platform which tossed and rolled, and offered a target alike for the whistling winds and the smarting spindrift. Presently the voice of Hogge spoke out of the blackness of the port end of the bridge.

'Jeff?'

'Aye, aye, Sir!' came a voice from the invisible forecastle.

'Tarpaulin the foc'sle skylight: it may yet burst.'

'Aye, aye, Sir!'

Hogge then ordered the two marines who were endeavouring to pace the promenade decks, to ascend to the bridge deck where they would be safer. The cruiser plunged and burrowed deeper and deeper into the waves, and in adition to those ahead, no sooner had they picked up the Saltings and thus left the lee of the north coast of Animalland than others, more vigorous in force and more bulky in volume, attacked them on the port side; and these latter type mounted higher and higher as the hours wore past, untill they dashed over the promenade and mounted almost to the level of the bridge deck.

Well was it that the care and foresight of Hogge had removed the marines from a post which they could not have maintained with safety. But there was yet another danger to be faced, and against this the lieutenant's ingenuity could form no plan. On either side of the bridge deck stood a light, quick-firing gun, and, as the waves mounted higher every time they hurled themselves with a reverberating crash against the deckhouse wall, it became evident to the watchful pig that they must soon reach to the guns, which, loosely constructed and lightly fastened on, could ill bear such a strain. He mentioned his fear to Cottle, and the cat descended from the bridge to order the marines to strengthen them by transvers lashings, he himself staying to assist in the work. It was a scene that in after life frequently recurred to the cat: the slippery deck reeling at an inconceivable angle, and covered with streams of water by each breaker: the three figures of himself and the marines working with almost superhuman energy to get their lashing finished before the waters rose to the hieght of the guns: and the faint outline of Hogge and the steersman far up in the high bridge.

Just as he bent to secure the last rope he caught a vision of a high, hoary-crested wave swooping down on him and on the gun. There was a crash, and he was buried in a world of green chilliness, and had a vague idea of being mixed up with the sharp corners and angles of the gun: he was carried over the far bulwark, and would have been buried in the boiling ocean had not the two marines siezed him by the arms and drawn him back. He staggered, dripping, to his feet, and, clutching to the half-submerged railings saw a twisted gap in the far bulwark, where the vicious wave had carried off the quick firing gun! His head rang, as if with some metallic blow.

'Are you all right, Cottle?' came the voice of Hogge from the darkness above.

'Yes, but the gun's gone,' panted the cat.

'Well come up to the bridge again and bring the marines with you. You can do no good down there.'

Before Cottle could obey or reply, he was bowled over again by a second wave. He felt himself kicking and being kicked by the two hapless marines. Next instant his head struck the bulwarks and he became insensible.

When Cottle revived, he found himself lying in a blanket before the saloon stove, with the commodore standing over him, holding in his hand a small bottle of brandy.

'All right?'

'Yes, thank you.'

'Good gracious! That was a night! It was bad enough when I came on at 3, but it must have been awful for you and Hogge.'

'I didn't know one got weather like that here.'

'Its the worst storm there's been for years.'

'Did the other quick firer go?'

'Yes. Bar, take Cottle to his cabin.'

As may be imagined, Cottle was in no wise sorry, even with Bar as his conductor, to seek his bunk, and forget his troubles in sleep.

CHAPTER VIII
THE SUGGESTION

For the next two days the unfortunate novice led a simple and placid life without moving from his bunk, the pity of himself and the envy of Bar. On the third day he was able to go and sit on the quarter-deck in a deck chair, and enjoy the calm weather, which was rendered all the more agreeable to him by contrast to that which he had at first experienced. While he was thus sitting, together with the watch below, namely the commodore's, which consisted of Wilkins & Macphail, Murray himself being in the saloon compiling his log. Of course Bar was present, since the worthy little paymaster stood no watch.

'By the way,' said Cottle, 'when we're not on voyague, how many gunnery practices do we have a week?'

'One,' said Wilkins. 'And quite enough it is.'

'Why?' returned Cottle, with surprise. 'Surely you like them.'

'Good Heavens! no,' said Wilkins. 'Whatever's the attraction?'

'Well,' said Cottle, 'there is all the excitement about the prize.'

'And about the detention,' said Bar.

'Yes,' laughed Wilkins, 'poor Bar always gets put down.'

'But,' said Cottle, 'one has to be a very, very bad shot for that.'

'Oh really!' ejaculated Bar with some warmth. 'We are much grieved that our shooting does not meet with the Alexandrian aproval!'

'But,' said Cottle to the company in general and ignoring the sarcasm, 'setting aside the question of Mr Bar, you can't deny that the educational value of a gunnery practice is undeniable.'

'Having your word for its being undeniable, we wouldn't dream of so doing,' said Macphail, who had been watching his mess-mates with the amused air of a philosopher watching children at play.

Cottle bridled.

'Being my official superior, Mr Macphail,' said he, 'I suppose you *HAVE* the right to jest at what is meant to be in earnest, but I must beg to disapprove of the taste which prompts you to do so.'

Macphail did not seem at all annoyed at this sally, but lent back in his chair and smiled obscurely at the clouds, while Bar openly chuckled. But Cottle bore in mind the scene at Riverside, and was not to be daunted from his heroic plan: he believed it was his mission in life to reform the Boxonian navy, and he meant to fulfill it. So he continued boldly.

'I'm going to ask Murray if we can have two a week, when we get home.'

Had a thunderbolt suddenly fallen on the quarter-deck of the *Greyhound*, the officers would have been scarcely more astounded. Bar dropped his lower jaw and gazed with horror at this 'viper they had been cherishing', as he told his friends afterwards: Wilkins, handsome, indulgent and lazy, laughed awkwardly: Macphail alone was unembarassed and smiled indulgently.

To break this unpleasant pause, came the clang of the bell for changing watch, and the officers filed off the quarter deck, leaving behind Bar and Cottle, for the latter had not yet returned to his duties.

'Cottle,' said Bar in a grave voice, 'will you come below and speak to me in my cabin for a few moments?'

'Certainly,' said Cottle, meaning exactly what he said. The bear rose and led the way through the saloon and down to his cabin.

Cottle followed with unsteady steps, and, as he went, he knew that the crisis was at hand: he realized that the long series of grudges stored up between himself and Bar had at last come to a head: that this was to be a battle between the old and the new.

And Bar fully appreciated these facts, and awaited with confidence a struggle in which he felt sure his superior wits and longer experience must be triumphant. One thing, however, was clear to him: he must not agravate his opponent to such an extent as to induce him to resort to his fists, for, as the shrewd paymaster was not slow to see, nothing but a painful and ignominious thrashing could be his share of such a 'contretemps'. Of course, even in this event, he had one refuge left, namely that of apealing to his fellow-officers against 'The vicious cat who had suddenly assaulted him in the middle of a friendly argument', and thus bring the force of public opinion to bear on his rival. But the coldness with which his complaints had been met by Hogge, and friendliness of Wilkins towards the interloper, showed him all too plainly that he would recieve but little support from his messmates: as well, if the quarrel were the property of the whole mess, it could scarce escape becoming that of the commodore also, and this was entirely at variance with Bar's schemes.

All these ideas, which flashed through the paymaster's brain at lightening speed, have taken some time to describe, but in reality the walk to Bar's cabin occupied less than a minute, so that Cottle, not so skilled or practiced as his adversary, had little time to arrange his plans, before the door was thrown open and he entered the lion's den.

Bar's cabin was, of course, the same in construction as any other, and yet it was different. The bulk of the bear's savings had gone to provide a large over-padded easy chair which formed the principle furniture of the apartment. The floor was littered over with books, coats, pamphlets and brown paper, so thickly that the carpet was quite invisible. The bunk was strewn with shore-going clothes, these last being the only articles in the room which were neatly placed and folded. The walls were covered with signed photo-graphs of actresses, intermingled with ones of the bear himself. Cottle felt he was at a disadvantage, and his enthusiastic young mind recieved an unwholesome impression of his rival's cabin.

CHAPTER IX
THE TURNING POINT

'Look here,' began Bar as soon as he had shut the door. 'This can't go on!'

'What do you mean?' said Cottle.

'I mean, that its either you or me manages this boat. Which is it to be?'

'I was not aware that either of us should.'

'What, then?'

'Surely, Commodore Murray is the master of the *Greyhound*.'

'Oh yes, of course,' said Bar wearily. 'But that's not what I meant.'

'Really, Mr Bar, you don't make yourself very plain.'

'I mean, to be simple, that either your ways or my ways must prevail.'

'What are your ways?'

'The opposite of yours! I don't want two gunnery days a week. I don't want a lot of rot about my duty. I can manage my duty alright, and I expect you to mind yours.'

'So I do. But I want the whole ship to be keen.'

'Keen on what?'

'Work and competition and that sort of thing.'

'What awful rot. And, as well, what business is it of yours?'

Cottle thought a minute, and, deciding it was time to play what he considered his trump card, said 'Do you really want to know?'

'Yes, of course, or I shouldn't ask!'

'Well then, listen: before we left Murry Lords Vant, Fortescue and Big interviewed me, and honoured me by commissioning me to reform this vessel.'

Cottle looked at Bar with a satisfied air, as if expecting the latter to fall to pieces and apologise, and was dissappointed to hear his adversary answer carelessly, 'But nobody takes any notice of that old kod Vant.' He knew well that these words destroyed his enemy's last support, and threw a whole volume of sarcasm and cruelty into the words, whose apparant carelessness was the outcome of polished art.

'It is a lie!'

'Oh,' said Bar with a debonair smile. 'And who does respect that dolorous bletherer?'

'Every Boxonian sailor who is true to his masters the kings, and under them to the admiralty! And you who – '

'Don't get angry,' said Bar with his diabolical skill in interrupting his opponent just when the latter was going to draw matters to a head, and, by a deliberate insult, compel the paymaster to resort to his fists. 'Pray, don't get angry! Let us discuss this matter like sane men. To return to the point, do you seriously intend to reform us?'

'I will try my best.'

'Oh! And have you started reforming the Commodore?'

'Your sarcasm is quite unnecessary. The Commodore is a man of honour, and I have no need to approach him.'

'The head of the Victualling Department . . . was kicked through his own . . . door.'

'Ah yes! A man of honour, and one who would kick you through his door, as I should, were you not just recovered from an illness.'

'Never mind the ilness. Try it.'

'I'm no fool,' said Bar, adopting the tone of a martyr. 'I know your game: you'll make me attack you and then talk to Murray about my striking weak, sick cats.'

'If you say that again,' said Cottle, towering over the little bear, 'I'll batter your ugly, varnish-colored snout till you look like a piece of mud – I mean till you look more like it than you do already!'

'But, to go back to the question of reform,' said Bar, who saw the argument getting into dangerous channels again, 'How were you going to go about it?'

'How "was" I? How AM I, you mean.'

'Oh, you're going to keep it up?'

'I see no reason to discontinue my efforts.'

'Look here,' said Bar. 'Drop it. Thats the advice of a man who has been at the game for fifteen years.'

'Yes. And what has he done in fifteen years?'

Bar shrugged his shoulders.

'What does anyone do?' he asked.

'His duty!' Cottle fired the words at his opponent, like so many cannon balls.

'What is duty?'

'Well, I suppose, work.'

'Well, I do enough work, at any rate.'

'You've never done a hand's turn.'

'And you, what have you done? Nothing except fool about melodramatically on the bridge deck.'

'I did my best.'

'Well, I've been doing my best for fifteen years.'

'I doubt it.'

'That does not change the fact.'

'Well, any way, what do you want with me down here? Eh?'

'I want to warn you to drop this absurd idea about reform: it won't work. And I've got the whole mess to back me up.'

It was a good lie, and went well.

'What can they do? And, I don't believe you have them.'

'Oh, rubbish!! But that is not the point: are you going to drop it?'

'No.'

[178]

'Well, then look out, young hero.'

'Alright. But, before I go, I must give you a few lessons, my fine hock brown.'

These words were a death knell to Bar's hopes of averting a hand to hand combat, and as he heard them he saw the brisk, well trained cat throw himself into a boxing attitude, whose correctness boded ill for the paymaster. In his long life in the navy – a life which was blotted by one or two ugly marks – Bar had acquired the habit of thinking very quickly, and it did not take him long to realize his position. He knew he had no chance of victory, nor even of safety, in an open fight, and hastily formed the plan of dashing in on his opponent, delivering one crushing blow, and escaping instantly through the door. Thus, and thus only, could the paymaster hope to escape the punishment he so richly deserved: in a long & evenly contested battle, clean living and the hard life of a naval college were sure to defeat self indulgence and unwholesome rotundity.

These thoughts flashed through the paymaster's brain in a few seconds, and (it seemed to Cottle) almost immeadiately he stood in a defensive posture. For a moment the two officers measured each other with their eyes, and then Cottle shot out a straight left-handed blow, which would have brought Bar to the ground, had not that worthy swerved aside, and delivered to his adversary a stinging punch on the nose. With this stroke, Bar turned and made for the door, but even as he did so, he realized that Cottle had grasped his maneouvre and was at his heels. One stride was enough to carry him across the room, and into the stride Bar concentrated all the power, speed and vigor of which his nature was capable. But his efforts were in vain! A relentless hand gripped the back of his collar & raised him off the ground, while a fierce vituperation rang in his hock-brown ears.

A moment later, Lieutenant James Bar, R.N., Paymaster and Head of the Victualling department, was ignominiously kicked through his own cabin door!

End of Volume One

"The deserters opened the window."

THE SAILOR
VOLUME II

CHAPTER X
THE RETURN

At the back of the Alhambra at the quiet little town of Danphabel there stands a low and small but snug villa, separated from the music hall only by a high-walled yard used for storing scenery, and having two pondorous gates, the one opening into a narrow street by which one approaches the stalls entrance, and the other onto the railway line. Many people think that this house is part of the music hall, in which opinion, although it is not actually correct, there is a considerable tincture of truth, for it is the residence of the manager, Mr Vorling. Nevertheless Mr Vorling does not at present occupy it, but has surrendured it to Viscount Puddiphat The Owl, who, being the owner of this and fourteen other music halls, has come down from Murry to give his subordinate a holyday, and to inspect this out of the way house, of which he knows comparatively little.

Viscount Puddiphat had long held the enviable title of the best dressed gentleman in Boxen, and to mantain and confirm this reputation was the object of the owl's life.

On a certain spring morning, the viscount's valet had entered his master's bed chamber with a cup of chocolate, and the ironed morning paper. No sooner had his step resounded on the floor than a mass of feathers stirred in the large bed, and the owl raised himself on his elbow, with blinking eyes. He was a well built bird of medium hieght, whose figure would have been of the finest, had it not been inclined to corpulence: his face was intellegent, and even handsome, and his curved beak shone like mahogany when the light caught: his expression was one of bland and unruffled benevolence, only occasionally to be fanned into temper or excitement, and his usual mode of expressing anger was by lending a scarcely audible tone of vexation to his mellow voice.

'Your chocolate, My Lord,' said the servant: the other took it, and, as he sipped it enquired what were the contents of the newspaper.

'The chief thing, My Lord, is that a cruiser called the *Greyhound* has dropped anchor in the bay this morning.'

'Ah,' said Puddiphat, half to himself and half aloud, 'I suppose my little friend James Bar will be onboard. Or was the *Ariadne* his boat? Anything else?'

'A long review of the Alhambra bill last night.'

'Favourable, I hope?'

'Yes, My Lord.'

The Viscount finished his chocolate in silence, and when he had dressed breakfasted at the local inn, repaired to the harbour for a stroll and a cigar on the jetty. As he was thus pleasantly employed, he noticed a spotless steam pinnace puting off from a large cruiser which lay at anchor in the offing, and which, as the pinnace drew nearer, he saw contained a person with whom he was well acquainted – namely Mr James Bar, a small hock-brown bear. This worthy stepped out of the pinnace as soon as it was alongside, and approached the bird arm in arm with a young cat, with whom he laughed and conversed freely and towards whom he displayed every sign of amity.

'Good morning, my dear Viscount,' said the bear. 'Allow me to introduce my friend Mr Cottle.'

'Delighted,' said Puddiphat. 'I suppose he's one of your desparate set. You are all desparadoes on the *Greyhound*.'

The two sailors exchanged an almost invisible glance, and Bar cast his bright, beady eyes downwards with a motion which might have been a nod, but which to the owl appeared as the very natural action of inspecting one's boots.

'Oh no,' said the bear gravely, 'we have had a change: Cottle has reformed us all.'

'Oh such nonsense, My dear Bar!' said the owl lightly. 'I was going to ask you and your friend to split a bottle of Zauber with me at my house to night, but I suppose you are above it.'

Bar's face displayed grave disapproval. ·

'Yes,' he said. 'But we shall be pleased to come and have the pleasure of your conversation, if not of your cellar.'

'You'll think differently by gas light, Bar,' replied the owl, 'but come any way – a few ladies are coming.'

'From the alhambra?' asked Bar severely.

'Yes. There's one – '

'My dear Viscount,' protested Bar, 'we must decline your hospitality if it entails mixing with these low actresses, whose presence recalls a chapter in our life, which we would fain forget.'

'This is Saul among the prophets,' laughed Puddiphat. 'But come along, the girls can dine at the inn.'

'Thank you,' said Bar. 'Good morning.'

'Good day, Mr Bar. But stay! How dare you wear that bright red tie? If I'd noticed it, I'd have cut you dead.'

'I'll change it. Good bye.'

The two friends bowed and walked on, leaving the owl in a meditative frame of mind. He had known the little hock-brown too long, and had helped him through too many desparate escapades, to believe in the sincerity of his reform, and yet the cat seemed just such a quiet and respectable person as might reprove the headstrong bear. And, he thought, if Bar had not really changed, he would have no object in pretending such an action, at least to a familiar friend like the Viscount.

While the owl was thus pondering, the two little animals who caused him such surprise and so excited his curiosity, were wending their way with linked arms towards the local admiralty lodge, whither they had been summoned by a telegram, on their arrival.

'But why,' Cottle was saying, 'Why keep it up before the Viscount, whom you describe as a trusty friend?'

'The Viscount is a gossip, and the news of my reform will have spread over the town in half an hour.'

'But, my dear Bar, the world at large isn't interested in your moral condition.'

'I daresay not: but in a place like Danphabel, anything is good enough to talk about.'

'Oh! Its a sleepy town?'

'Very. But Cottle – ?'

'Yes.'

'How ever shall I keep it up? There's the inn over there, and I want a bottle of Vin-de-Brus. I may give way any moment.'

'For heaven's sake don't,' cried the other. 'Once a saint always a saint!'

'Dear, Dear, yes! But think of the strain! It was far better in the old days, before Macphail persuaded you to drop your reform idea! And, why should

[183]

I pose as a reformed character?'

'Don't you see,' said the cat in alarm, 'I can't go back to the admiralty with nothing to show: I can't tell them I've given it up. And, as well, it will be for your own benefit, to keep in Vant's favour.'

'Here is the admiralty,' said Bar.

The two conspirators stopped outside a big, over-ornamented building, and, obeying the sonorous 'Come in!' which answered their knock, entered the porch.

CHAPTER XI
THE INTERVIEW

Bar and Cottle were met by a grave tortoise who ushered them into a stuffy little office, panelled in unvarnished deal, and divided down the middle by a wooden rail, behind which sat three persons whose greatness would have made Bar shiver in his shoes, had not the little bear been too busily engaged in assuming an expression of penitence and humility. They were, in point of fact, Lord Vant, first Lord of the Admiralty, Marshal Fortescue, Head of the War Office, and Lord Big, Little-Master. The two sailors bowed and remained silent.

'Well,' said Lord Big, 'and how has my colleague's plan worked?'

'I can almost foretell the answer,' said Fortescue scornfully. 'It is a failure, it is impracticable.'

'Your Lordship is wrong,' returned Cottle. 'True, it is uphill work, but I have had some success.'

Vant's benevolent countenance softened into a smile of childish glee.

'Ah, my good little kitten,' he said. 'I knew it, I knew it!'

'Be quiet Vant,' said the Little-Master in a hurried whisper, and added aloud, 'And what is this progress, Mr Cottle?'

'My friend Mr Bar, is a convert,' said Cottle proudly.

'Convert to what?' said Fortescue sharply.

'To good living, and to an attempt to reform the navy.'

'Oh!' said Fortescue, casting a piercing glance on the cat. 'And how did you convert him?'

'By hard fighting, M'Lord. We were much at variance at first.'

'To be sure,' returned the Marshal. 'And what do you intend to do while you are in port?'

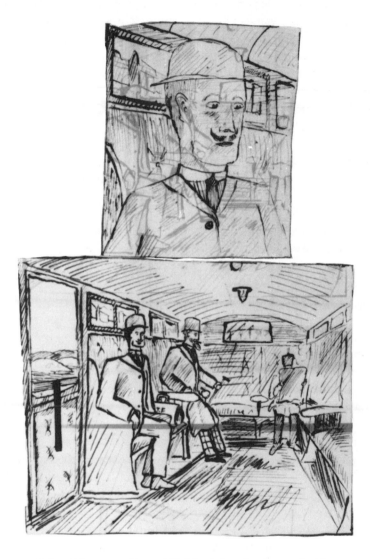

Colonel Fortescue, General Quicksteppe and an huzzar inside a
Piscian State Railway Saloon.

'Enjoy a few days rest and amusement My Lord.'

'And what form does this amusement take? For instance, what are you doing to night?'

Cottle opened his mouth to speak and shut it again, and turned red beneath his glossy fur, shooting furtive glances at his accomplice.

'I – I don't know that we're doing anything, My Lord,' he stammered.

Bar's face never changed.

'Oh!' said Fortescue. 'Have you met any friends since you came in?'

Cottle was miserable. He dared not reveal the compromising dinner to which they were resolved to go, and where, despite their protestations they were determined to do full justice to the wines and society provided: on the other hand he could not tell how much this sharp little soldier knew, who, as far as Cottle knew, might have been among the crowd who were taking a morning stroll on the jetty, and might have heard their whole conversation with the music hall potentate.

'Oh yes, a few, My Lord,' he replied with studied (somewhat too studied) indiference.

'Oh! Who?'

'Well – er – Viscount Puddiphat.'

'Oh, you know him? Well, you are lucky! And where did you meet him?'

'On the jetty.'

'Did you converse long?'

'No, I did not,' said Cottle whose temper was going.

'And what did he talk about? I suppose he invited you somewhere? He nearly always has something on.'

'Really, My Lord, I don't feel called upon to answer such private questions.'

'Quite right,' said the Little-Master who had been growing impatient during his colleague's examination. Turning to the latter he added, 'And, I confess, Fortescue, I don't see the point of this cross examination.'

'Curiosity, merely curiosity, my dear Little-Master!'

'You may go,' said Lord Big to the two victims.

As soon as they once more were out in the narrow street up which the sea breeze was blowing as through a funnel, Cottle fell onto rather than sat upon a public bench and gasped.

'Good heavens!' he sighed. 'That was awful.'

'Yes,' agreed Bar, sitting beside him. 'But you managed him quite well

– for a beginner.'

'Oh, it was awful. I can't stand another inquisition like that!'

'You'll have to learn if we are to play a winning game.'

'No, its too bad! I am going to go back and tell them its all humbug, and lump the results. Anything is preferable to – '

'For goodness' sake don't! You'll brand yourself as the biggest liar in the navy, and perhaps get shot out, or at least get into an awful plight. We must see it through now.'

'That fellow Fortescue will have us yet. I can see that coming.'

'Oh no he won't: I'll play through him like a trout. Only mind, we're saints.'

'Oh dear! Why ever did we get into a mess like this?'

'Because you stopped reforming.'

'Well that couldn't have gone on!'

'Certainly not. But, we're still alright. You needn't give up, Cottle. Only it is a strain. Come and have a glass of – soda-water.'

CHAPTER XII
THE CURTAINED RECESS

Cottle and Bar stood at Puddiphat's door in evening dress.

'Shall we go in?' said Bar.

'Is it safe?' asked Cottle.

'Well, I don't see why not.'

'Shall we?'

'Yes.'

The little bear rang the bell and was shown into a narrow hall, whose size conveyed an impression of poverty, which was everywhere contradicted by the tastful and expensive decorations. Passing through the door which a manservant held open on the left, they found themselves in a small dining room, furnished in the Turkish style, which is to day so popular in Boxen among persons connected with the stage. There were a few chairs, and a great many low, soft divans, and a huge fire was burning in the grate although it was a warm night in April. The occupants of the room were the Viscount himself and an old man, whose snowy beard covered his shirt front and rivaled it in whiteness, but whose eyes twinkled with life & merriment.

'Allow me,' said Puddiphat, 'to introduce his Excellency General Quick-steppe. General, Cottle & Bar, two naval friends.'

Cottle stared! Were the tales that were told of the General's habit of slipping away from court to join doubtful gatherings, true? And was this indeed the famous soldier?

'Come, Cottle,' said the owl, 'the general doesn't bite. Sit down.'

'By the way,' said Bar, 'tell us when its quarter to eleven.'

The host promised, and, after a few more guests had arrived, the meal began, when it became noticeable that neither of Puddiphat's promises, in connection with wines or actresses had been carried out, a fault which, it must be said, the two guests forgave over-easily. Thus the hours sped swiftly by, and the young cat and his mentor were held entranced by the conversation of the gay owl and his theatrical friends.

Suddenly it happened!

It always does happen suddenly, whether it is the murder of the heroine, or the opening of an overture at an opera, or one's bow tie slipping. But it was none of these calamities which so distressed the bear and his friend: it was merely the commonplace occurrence of the hour of twelve striking.

'Good Heavens,' ejaculated Bar in a sepulchral tone as the last stroke ceased to vibrate. 'The *Greyhound* sailed an hour ago.'

'Well,' said the owl, 'does it matter?'

'Matter!! Of course! We shall be tried as deserters.'

'Dear, Dear!' said Puddiphat. 'I don't know what you'd better do.'

'You confounded fool,' said Bar angrily, 'I told you to remind us.'

'It is no time for quarrelling now,' said the owl calmly. 'I'm as badly off as you. When the affair comes out, I shall come under the arm of the law, for aiding and abetting a deserter. It is too late to do anything now: so split another bottle and forget our danger.'

'Here! Here!' cried Cottle, mounting on his chair, and seeking to drown his fears in the bottle of rare old Middlehoff which he brandishes above his head. 'To the health of liberty!'

'Liberty!' shouted the mingled company, and everyone re-filled their glasses, with a hearty laugh.

'To morrow,' said Bar, 'I don't care what happens. Let us live for to night.' And with this excellent maxim he sank onto a sofa and dashed off another glass.

Puddiphat alone was miserable. He had seen many such carousals before, and knew their results: he leant back in his chair, and gazed on every guest, and sighed wearily. It was no use! The morning must come, and with it retribution. He himself would see the interior of a jail for this, and so would the deserters. As he was reflecting thus, the door was flung open and a butler announced 'His Lordship The Little Master and Marshal Fortescue, on urgent business.'

Silence fell on all, except Bar, who, either because of the fumes of the palatable liquid which he had imbibed, or because of his natural courage, continued the song he was singing with redoubled vehemence.

'Shut up, you d—d fool!' cried the terrified owl. 'They're just coming.'

'I don't care,' chuckled Bar. 'I know the Little Master. He's a good fellow – so's Fortescue, so's everybody.'

'Here they come,' cried the agonized Viscount. 'Quick, get into that recess and draw the curtains.'

The place indicated was a narrow, panelled imbrasure, containing an oaken settle, and across whose front two baize curtains might be drawn. Cottle, seeing his only refuge, siezed his biblulous friend, and drew the curtains to conceal their furtive forms, just as the door opened to admit the two politicians.

'Good evening, My dear Little-Master, and you My Lord Marshall,' said Puddiphat, rising and coming forward, and conveying by his manner the impression that the presence of these newcomers was all he required to make him happy. 'This is indeed an honour.'

'If you were to wish us good morning, Viscount,' returned Fortescue coldly, 'it would be more correct: we have come on a most distasteful errand.'

'The errand which bringes your Lordships under my poor roof, has done good to me at least,' said the owl unctiously.

'No waste to time,' said Fortescue, ignoring the compliment, 'I may as well tell you that we suspect you of entertaining a certain bear and cat who should be at present on board his majestie's ship *Greyhound*, and wish to search the house.'

'Bear and cat?' retorted the owl in a puzzled tone. 'This is not a mena-garie.'

'No,' said Fortescue. 'Will you let me pass?'

'I really don't see why I should submit to this indignity.'

'I am sorry Viscount, but in the interests of justice, I must request your obedience.'

'Well, the door behind you opens into my bedroom, the only other apartment besides this and the servant's quarters.'

'Stop!' said the Little-Master who up till now had been engaged in rebuking Quicksteppe with whom he was intimately acquainted. 'What is behind those curtains?'

'An empty recess,' said Puddiphat without moving a muscle of his handsome face.

'Ah, well why are the curtains drawn?' said the Little-Master suspiciously, and, before any one could intercept him, he rushed up, drew back the curtains, and found – an empty space.

CHAPTER XIII
THE ULTIMATUM

A quick flicker of intellegence passed over the Viscount's face, unobserved by the two politicians who stood glaring at the empty recess, as if at a dangerous beast.

'Well, Gentlemen,' he said, seating himself on the settle. 'You see, I sometimes speak the truth.'

'Always, My dear Viscount,' said Fortescue blandly. 'Accept our apologies.'

'All the same,' said the Little-Master uneasily, 'we haven't got to the bottom of this matter yet.'

'Do you still persist in your odious insinuations?' said Puddiphat without rising.

'Oh, of course I take your word,' said the Little-Master, 'but all the same I don't think this mystery is solved.'

'Really, My Lord, your conversation is either intentionally insolent or foolishly tactless. Your hat is on the peg in the hall.'

'Come on, Fortescue,' said the frog, in a tone which implied an unwillingness to stay longer in such a company, and the two baffled politicians left the house. At their departure, the owl neither rose from his seat nor displayed any relief, but continued his polite conversation as if no interruption had occurred, and his guests, divining that he wished to be alone, made their adieux, and departed.

No sooner had the door closed on the last reveller than the owl sprang up, and, lifting the lid of the settle on which he had been seated, helped out two very weary and cramped figures who proved to be Bar and Cottle.

'Faugh!' exclaimed the bear. 'How often is the inside of that place cleaned? I was nearly choked with the dust!'

'Be thankful you are not inspecting the inside of a prison,' said the owl gravely. 'And now, it will be safer for you to leave this house.'

'We will not trespass on your hospitality much longer,' said Bar, 'but let me just have a bottle of Middlehoff, to clear my throat.'

'No, No,' said the owl, interposing himself between his guest and the bottles. 'You are sober now: remain so.'

'Look here,' said Cottle wearily. 'Won't the Little-Master and Fortescue be about in the street?'

'Very well,' said the owl. 'This window opens onto the railway: get through it.'

'Good bye, Viscount.'

'Good bye. No – no more Middlehoff, Mr Bar,' cried the owl, as the bibulous little hock brown showed signs of approaching the table.

With this terse farewell, the two deserters opened the window, and passed out, to find themselves on a narrow strip of land, covered with rank grass, and lying between the music hall and the railway line. A thin, drenching rain was falling; and, in the uncertain light of dawn, they distinguished a tall figure, wrapped in a cloak who eyed them fiercely as he passed, causing the guilty sailors to shiver with fear. After a few moments a light appeared, and a long goods train lumbered into view, puffing and panting like an animal in pain.

'Come on,' whispered Bar. 'Its our only chance to get away before morning.'

'Board her?'

'Yes.'

They stood waiting till a conveniently low truck passed, and, at the right moment, caught the edge firmly, and, with a terrifing sensation of heaving ground, swung themselves up and sank down breathless among the coals.

They had hardly accomplished this difficult, not to say dangerous feet, when there was a squealing of brakes and the long train came to a standstill.

[191]

Bar, peering over the edge with intense caution saw a knot of dark figures, who were presently joined by the engineers of his own train. Each man was armed with a heavy club, and from the stealth of the meeting and the midnight hour, the bear could argue only some desparate purpose. At first the consultation was held in whispers, whose purport was none the less terrible because it was half hidden. At last, the foremost villain, who held a lamp, which revealed his fierce and bearded face, exclaimed, 'Ah, have done with your talkin' an' pother! Come to something! Do you mean to strike or do yer nut?'

'We do,' cried a chorus of hoarse voices.

'Aye, an' its right ye are! In the old days, the raily men did what work they liked, & none more. Were they any better than we?'

'No!' came the chorus.

'No,' repeated the speaker, refreshing himself from a heavy jug. 'A thousan' times – No! An' we will nut do it, either. This new stashun master, has a wrong noshun. He takes his men fer beasts of the field! An' will we stan' it?'

'No!' thundered the others.

'Then strike! Let him know he cant do without us! Do we mind work?' – the chorus seemed disposed to return an affirmative but the orator continued – 'No! But we mind tyrranny!! What is our password?'

An indistinct murmer came from the crowd, who seemed hazy on this point.

'Yes!' cried the scandalist. ' "Danphabel, with its thousand colored copulas." Do nut ferget it. Now, leave the train, an' come. No more work! No more tyranny!'

This cheerful prospect was greeted by the crowd with loud huzzahs, and they rapidly dispersed, waving their cudgels above the heads, and elevating the orator to their shoulders, where that worthy was fully acquainted with the penalties of fame.

'Good gracious,' cried Bar, turning to the cat. 'A strike on the railway! We cannot get away!'

CHAPTER XIV
THE PRODIGALS' RETURN

Commodore Murray awoke next morning with an uneasy feeling that something disagreeable had happened over night, whose exact nature he could not remember. The feeling so grew upon him as he dressed that, when he entered the saloon for breakfast, he no longer wondered if a catastrophe had occured but merely wished to know what it was.

'Good morning, gentlemen,' he said cheerfully, and then added, glancing round, 'Bar not here?' The occupants of the room suddenly became very much more interested than usual in their cofee, but no word was spoken. The Commodore was annoyed, and silently took his seat and tried to read the paper: but he could not fix his attention on the lurid headings, and as the meal went on he became even more restless.

'Where is Bar?' he asked at length, turning to Macphail. 'And Cottle isnt here either?'

'I didnt see them last night at all, after we came on board,' returned the engineer.

'What! Did they not come on board?'

'I didn't see them.'

'Well,' exclaimed Murray, now thoroughly roused. 'Why the devil didn't you tell me?'

'Commodore,' said the old enginner, 'we've sailed together for seven years now, and I have always been your friend: you have always been mine. But how was this brought about? Not by my bearing through to you every secret of my fellows! And now, even for a friend, I shall not turn informer.'

The grizzled cynic of the engine-room had shown more feeling than was his wont, and the other was passified: still, however, restless and annoyed, he left the room and paced the quarter deck. Bar and Cottle, if found, must be shown up and pay the penalty: it was no use, even had he wished it, to try and shield them: and he would lose two officers whom he had always liked, and it would not redound to the ship's credit. As he was thus ruminating a rowing boat drew up alongside and the portly person of the harbour master stepped on board. The worthy official was somewhat perturbed and explained in lurid terms how a railway strike had occurred on shore: Murray listened with polite attention, inwardly wondering why he was favoured with this confidence; at last he said 'Thank you, Harbour-master, for your news. Can I help you in any way?'

'No: but I fancy I can be of use to you.'

'How?'

'Two of your officers – '

'Yes!'

' – Mr Bar and Mr Cottle, I believe, missed the sailing of your pinnace.'

'Quite right.'

'They are at present in my office, and they have asked me to speak to you. It was by no means their fault in being late: on the contrary they suffered, like many others, from the strike. The 2 gentlemen had passed their afternoon in going for a trip to the next station down the line, and, owing to the suspension of traffic were unable to return.'

'Thank you,' said Murray heartily, and in his heart he thanked his stars both then and that afternoon when the two deserters came onboard under cover of an obvious lie, yet one which Murray was ready to accept for the good of the ship. And so it befell that our two friends had reason to bless that strike which a few hours before had seemed to sound the death knell of their hopes. They have since been good friends if not good officers and they manage to hit off a golden mean between Bar's desparate exploits and Cottle's absurd idealism.

ENCYCLOPEDIA
BOXONIANA

INTRODUCTION

I *The Plan of the Encyclopedia*

The writer of a complete Boxonology – a work which is still to be attempted – would have two sources of almost equal value on which to base his researches; on the one hand, the surviving documents, and on the other, the oral tradition. The aim of this encyclopedia is to reduce to a serviceable form the first of these two sources, by tabulating all that can be known of Boxen and the Boxonian world from the documentary sources alone; the documents including, besides Texts proper, the various Maps, Plans, and Pictures. With this end in view, it clearly became my duty to exclude everything that rests upon tradition: not because I regarded the tradition as invariably less reliable than the documents, but because a digest of tradition is obviously work that could not be undertaken single-handed, and, if undertaken, could have no undisputed authority. For similar reasons I have been sparing of conjecture and inference. To draw out all that can be deduced from the texts, to attempt the solution of all problems and the removal of all contradictions in the light of general probability and skilful hypothesis, would have been to anticipate the future Boxonologist rather than to provide him with his tools.

A further limitation has still to be noticed, and it is one that turns upon the peculiar nature of the subject matter. When we approach the history and structure of the terrestrial world, we have no difficulty in distinguishing between its outward or phenomenal character – its events and natural conditions, which we hand over to the scientist – and its ultimate source and meaning, which we assign to the theologian and the philosopher. The one is matter of knowledge, the other of faith or speculation. In the Boxonian world, on the contrary, both are alike, for us, matters of knowledge. Those facts outside the world that appeared to the Boxonians, on which, nevertheless, that world depended; its origins and destiny, and the process whereby its characters or 'souls' came into being: everything, in short, which to the Boxonians themselves (had they known it) would have constituted their religion or their metaphysic, will be mere matter of memory to the readers of this encyclopedia. And this matter is of absorbing interest; to trace the process by which an attic full of commonplace childrens' toys became a world as consistent and self-sufficient as that of the Iliad or the Barsetshire novels, would be no small contribution to general psychology. But such a work, again, demands collaboration. The solitary memory is defective: and even where it seems to remember, it cannot claim authority. I have therefore confined myself to such an account of Boxen as a well informed Boxonian himself could have given.

II *The Documents*

In approaching the work my first business was necessarily to draw up an exhaustive list of all surviving documents and to estimate their comparative value. I had believed that memory alone was sufficient to furnish me with the list: but the discovery of *four* fragmentary histories of Animalland, where I had remembered only two, soon warned me of my mistake. Having thus been forced to abandon memory as an absolute test, I was reduced to search – a method which has the disadvantage of leaving us always uncertain whether some document has not been overlooked. At the same time, I am of opinion that no Text of first rate importance was ever forgotten. Fragments and short monographs, individual drawings and sketch maps, may still wait to be discovered and to enlighten us on matters of detail. A *Supplement to the Encyclopedia* may thus, at any time, become necessary: but the main outlines of the Boxonian world (with one great exception) are fixed beyond dispute.

The following list of Texts will also serve as a key to the references in the Encyclopedia. I have prefixed to each Text the initial letters by which it is referred to, and the reader should make himself familiar with these before he proceeds. (The arabic numerals, which follow the initial letters in references, indicate the page of the Text in question: the Roman numerals, where necessary, indicate the volume. Thus 'LB II 13' means '*Life of Big*. Volume II. page 13'. References to chapters, or (in plays) to Acts and Scenes, are not made use of in the Encyclopedia.)

List of Texts

1. KR = *The King's Ring*. Found in a small account book with stiff black covers. Almost certainly the oldest text which we have, it

deals, in a crude, archaic fashion, with the theft of the crown jewels of Animalland by James Hit, in the reign of Benjamin I.

2. TS = *Tom Saga*. I have given this name, for purposes of reference, to an un-named narrative dealing with the exploits of the heroes Bob, Tom and Dorimie, against the Cats. It is very archaic in style and must have been written not long after KR. It is sewn up inside the cover of a yellow limp-backed account book together with the next Text: the cover bearing the joint title 'Tales of Mouseland'.

3. GG = *The Glorious Goal*. An unfinished narrative dealing with the adventures of the Jaspers and of Benjamin I in Tararo. It shows a great advance in style and structural power and gives valuable confirmation to the more strictly historical Texts.

4. OH = *Old History*. (So called for purposes of reference; the MS. bears the title *History of Mouseland from Sto' A to Bub I*, i.e. from Stone-age to Bublish I.) Found in a small account book with limp black covers. An unfinished history of Mouseland. It does not descend lower than the Indian Settlement, contradicts all known history, and is nearly worthless. In style it is as archaic as TS, and may be earlier than GG.

5. LH = *The Lost History*. (So called because it was unexpectedly discovered in the attic in 1927. In the MS, the title is *History of Mouseland*.) Found in an exercise book with limp yellow covers. It comes down to the reign of an apocryphal Bublish II, and is generally inconsistent with the better histories, though recording some valuable facts. In style and spelling it suggests a date slightly earlier than GG.

6. MH = *Middle History*. (So called for purposes of reference. The MS. bears the ambitious title *History of Animalland from 1327 to 1906*.) Found in a quarto exercise book with limp yellow covers very much defaced by scribbling. Alone among our texts it is written in pencil. It gives a clear and credible account of

Animallandic History from the landing of the Indians to the latter half of the reign of Benjamin I. It disagrees with OH and LH, but is in entire agreement with NH, which sometimes reproduces it word for word.

7. NH = *New History.* (In the MS, *History of Animalland.*) Found in an exercise book, very small quarto, with limp terra cotta covers. In range, style, and credibility, it is easily the best of the Histories, and brings us down as far as the Lantern Act. The writer apparently has KR, TS, GG, and MH before him and has some idea of the historical handling of sources. In his treatment of the Feline War (NH 16-18) he regards himself as giving a *historical* account of the same events which TS treats in the epic and fabulous manner.

8. CHM = *The Chess Monograph.* (Un-named in the MS.) A short narrative of four pages, found in the same book with OH, and describing the *risorgimento* of the Chess under Flaxman, and the foundation of the first Chessarics. It is in almost complete agreement with the account of the same events given in NH 23 *et seq*,[1] and appears to be a little earlier.

9. MCH = *The Murry Chronicle.* One number only of this paper has been discovered. It consists of an uncovered sheet of notepaper and contains an account of the origin and outbreak of the Pongeein War in the reigns of Hawki IV and Benjamin VI. It seems to have been written later than NH and CHM.

10. MET = *The Murry Evening Telegraph.* Eleven numbers of this paper have been found. Numbers 1 to 6 are sewn together in a cover decorated with paintings. The remaining numbers are loose. It gives an account of daily events in the reigns of *Benjamin VI* and *Hawki IV* at a period shortly after the Pongeein War, and

---

[1] The reader will notice that KR, TS, GG, MH, NH, and CHM, by their substantial agreement with one another, establish themselves as first class texts, and at the same time degrade OH and LH to the level of 'bad' texts.

is a mine of valuable information. It is certainly later than MCH.[1]

11. B = *Boxen*. Found in two exercise books with limp terra cotta covers. This narrative, in the form of a novel, deals primarily with the history of Orring's League in the early years of *Hawki V* and *Benjamin VII*, and the political rise of Polonius Green. It is much later than MET.

12. LD = *The Locked Door*. Found in a Malvern exercise book with half-limp black covers. This text is also in the form of a novel, and deals with the Tracity War. The writer has B before him and has connected the events he describes with those described in B.

13. SS = *The Sailors*. Found in two exercise books with limp blue covers. A novel, dealing almost exclusively with the life of naval officers on T.M.S. Greyhound, and therefore of less value than B and LD for the study of Boxonian life and institutions in general. Many characters, however, are common to it and them, and all three texts tend to confirm one another.

14. LB = *Life of Big*. Found in three small notebooks (Malvern) with limp black covers. The author, starting at 1856, brings his narrative down to 1913. For much of his matter he is our only authority, but elsewhere confirms NH, MCH, B, LD and SS.

15. THK = *Than Kyu*. Found in the same book with LD. This short narrative relates an otherwise unknown episode of Big's early life.

16. LSM = *Littera Scripta Manet*. Found in an exercise book with limp yellow covers. This text gives in dramatic form an account of

[1] In references to MET the numeral refers to the 'Number' of the paper, not to the page. Careless duplications of number in the original have forced me to number the *loose* METs thus; – 7, 7A, 8, 9, 9A.

the reconciliation between James Bar and Big, and is in agreement with the story of the same event given in LB III 21 *et seq.*

17. UP = *Unfinished Play.* Found in an exercise book with limp yellow covers, which has since been utilised as the 2nd volume of *Leeborough Studies.* It deals with an attempt of Big's to induce Quicksteppe to marry. Only one act has been completed. The episode is nowhere else recorded: but the general framework and the characters are in agreement with LB, LD, B etc.

18. LS = *Leeborough Studies.* A series of drawings of all periods collected in two exercise books with limp yellow covers. The Boxonological section often represents episodes recorded in the Texts and provides portraits of many important characters. (References indicate the number of the Plate by a Roman numeral.)

The Boxonian Apocrypha

Under this heading I have grouped together a number of texts which refer to the Boxonian world but which cannot, for various reasons, be regarded as giving trustworthy evidence about it. It should be remembered, however, that all these texts may occasionally supply written evidence for events well attested by tradition, or rendered extremely probable by the better texts. Where they are our only authorities, their statements, if intrinsically probable, may be accepted, though with caution. The Apocrypha includes the following texts; –

I. THE SQUIRREL FRAGMENT (SQF). An unfinished narrative dealing with the adventures of a free company under the leadership of the squirrel Strawbane, against the Cats. Its style suggests a date rather later than GG, and it is found in a quarto exercise book

[A page of the *Encyclopedia* was torn out here. There is enough of it left to show that it contained writing on both sides. Besides losing a list of the Boxonian Aprocrypha, we no longer have what were the dates of 'Period I' of section III – *Chronology.* The *Encyclopedia* continues as follows:]

PERIOD II *or* GREAT HIATUS: Early Boxen down to 1856.
  (No sources.)

PERIOD III: 1856–1913.
  (*Sources:* – MCH, MET, B, LD, SS, LB, THK, LSM, UP.)

PERIOD I. – NH abstains from all attempt at chronology. The remaining histories, from the chronological point of view, fall into two families; –
  (a) OH and LH which assign the Indian settlement and the unification of Calico to the early thirteenth century.
  (b) MH which gives 1327 for the accession of Hacom and unification of Calico, and 1340 for the death of Benjamin I.
  Evidence exists in favour of the B-chronology. We know that the defeat of the Cats occurred in the reign of King Mouse the Good who succeeded Benjamin I (NH 15–17). We also know that King Mouse was 'old' and 'worn out with anxiety' when he died 'soon after' the conclusion of the Feline War (*ibid.*, 18). We may therefore assume that he had a long reign. If we accept 1340 for the death of Benjamin I, and forty years for the reign of King Mouse, we shall have 1380 for King Mouse's death and 1375–79 for the defeat of the Cats. So much for the B-chronology.
  If we now turn to LB II 13 we shall find it stated that the defeat of the Cats took place 'over five hundred years before' the Emancipation Bill of 1897; which would bring it, say, to 1390. Thus LB and the B-chronology agree within fifteen years in their date for the Feline War, which implies a similar agreement as to the dates of Benjamin I and Mouse the Good, while the A-chronology would disagree with both by a century. When we add to this the general inferiority of OH and LH, in which the A-chronology is given, we need have no hesitation in accepting the B-chronology.
  As MH does not come lower than Benjamin I, and NH gives no dates, we have no chronology offered for the later history of Pre-Boxonian Animalland. It is not impossible, however, to arrive at an approximate date for the Union. We know from LB I 10 that Danphabel School was founded by Bublish II 'three hundred years' before Big entered it in 1870: *i.e.* in 1590. We also know (*ibid.*) that Little-Master White was educated at Danphabel: and, that the same White (NH 32) was Little-Master under Bublish II at the time of the Union. He therefore had time to grow up and climb to the Little-Magisterial chair in the lifetime of the King who founded the school

at which he was educated. We are, further, entitled to assume, on the analogy of terrestrial history, that the school-going age was younger in the Sixteenth, than in the Twentieth, century. If White has been one of the first pupils to enter Danphabel when it was founded in 1570, and if he had then been 6 years of age, he would not have been thirty till 1593: and as it is very unlikely that he would have become Little-Master at an earlier age, we may therefore be sure that the Union took place either in 1593 or later. Again, Bublish II, who was not born in the purple and had to fight for the crown, cannot have been in a position to found Danphabel before his twenty-fifth year. Assuming that he was twenty-five at the time of the foundation (*i.e.* in 1570), 1630 – when he would have been eighty-five – is the latest year which we can, with any probability, assume for his death: and as he certainly survived the Union by a year or so (NH 33) its date cannot be later than 1628. I therefore conclude that the Union took place sometime between 1593 and 1628: 1610 may be regarded as a convenient date which cannot be seriously wrong.

Before leaving the 1st Period, a word should be said of the Pre-Historic period; by which I mean to include such events as the texts occasionally allude to, which come before the beginning of connected narrative in the Histories. The earliest historical fact of which the texts hold any record is the existence of a Piscian empire, ruled by one Pau-Amma, and described by Big (LD 21) as flourishing in a high state of civilisation two centuries before the Pongeein invasion of Animalland. NH, which alone of the histories knows anything of the Pongeein period, gives no dates: but we can work back from the B-chronology of MH. Hacom's Porcine expedition took place in 1329 (MH 2), shortly after his third annual council (NH 3) and therefore in the fourth year of his reign. This fixes Hacom's accession at 1325. The earliest Indian settlements took place about a century earlier (NH 2), and are described as being 'the first notable event' after the Pongeein evacuation: which suggests the first years of the thirteenth century for the fall of the Pongeein empire in Animalland. NH 1 and LD 21 both make it clear that the Pongeeins not only conquered the country but held it for some time as part of their empire. As we have no means of determining the duration of this Pongeein period, and know only that the Piscian empire flourished two centuries before its commencement, we cannot provide a *terminus post quem* for Pau Amma. What we are able to conclude is that he cannot have lived later than the middle of the eleventh century.

PERIOD II. – Since the Great Hiatus begins immediately after the troubles arising in connection with the Lantern Act (NH 33), that is, in the early years of the seventeenth century, and ends with the beginning of LB in 1856, we can now determine its extent as roughly two hundred and fifty years. In the absence of any connected account of this period we are reduced to collecting scattered references to isolated events from the texts of the III^d Period and from the apocryphal MCC. These, with their dates, will be given in the Chronological Table below.

PERIOD III. – For the greater part of this period we have simply to copy down the dates given in LB. After the accession of *Benjamin VII* and *Hawki V* in 1908, our chronological problem is the comparatively simple one of fitting into the framework of LB the events recorded in B, LD, SS, THK, LSM and UP.

On the following page I have attempted a chronological table. The dates are largely based on LB.

IV *Chronological Table*

PERIOD I

XIth Century	*Piscian* empire of *Pau–Amma*.
1200	Decline of *Pongeein Empire*. *Pongeein* evacuation of *Animalland*.
	Indian settlements in *Mouseland*.
	Alliance of *Indian* settlers with the *Cosois*.
1325	*Hacom* crowned King of all *Calico*.
	Foundation of the *Damerfesk*.
1329	*Hacom's Porcine* war; and death.
1330	Accession of *Bublish I*.
1331	Assassination of *Bublish I*. Accession of *Benjamin*.
	Discovery of *Tararo*.
	A '*Hawkie*' reigning in *India*.
	Union of *Southern Animalland* with *Calico*.
	Reform of the *Damerfesk*.
1340	Death of *Benjamin I*. Accession of *King Mouse*.
1375	Suppression of *Feline* resolt. *Feline* disabilities imposed.

[204]

1380   Death of *King Mouse*. Formation of *Commonwealth*.
Democratic rising and dictatorship of *Balkyns*.
Rise of *Perrenism*.
Death of *Balkyns*. Commonwealth continued, but power reverts
     to the middle classes. *Leppi I* becomes '*governer*'.
Rise of the *Chessaries*.
Persecution of *Perrenism*.
Death of *Leppi I*. Accession of *Leppi II*.
Foundation of the *Clique*. Abolition of *Slavery* in *Animalland*.
Monarchist rising in the South of Animalland. Death of Leppi
     II.
Restoration of *monarchy* by the *Damerfesk*.
1560–70 (?)   Accession of *Bublish II*.
Foundation of office of Little-Master.
1610   Union of *Animalland* with *India*.
Attempted abolition of *Slavery* in *India*.
The *Lantern Act*.

PERIOD II

circ. 1790   Floruit the *Sly Italian* in *Animalland*.
1800   Floruit *Hawk Wages* in *India*.
1801   Abolition of *Slavery* in *India*.
1848   Lord *Robert Big's Domestic Servants Act*.
1854   The elder *Chutney* born.

PERIOD III

1856   Lord *John Big* born.
1870   He enters *Danphabel*.
1874   Leaves *Danphabel*.
1876   Enters *Great Eglington*.
1879   Is called to the *bar*. (Visits *Than Kyu?*)
1881   Becomes *Cornet of Dragoons*.
1883   Death of Lord *Robert Big*.
1884   Shops *Hours* Act. Murry *riots*.
1885   Train outrage in *Pongee*.
1886   (*Jan.*) War with *Pongee* declared.

[205]

	(*March*) *Pongeein* expedition sails.
	Siege of *Fortressa*.
1888	Relief of *Fortressa*. March on *Omaar-Raam*.
1890	Lord *John Big's* dash to the coast.
1892	He becomes member of *Damerfesk*.
1893	Peace with *Pongee*.
1895	Marquis of *Calcutta's* budget. The affair of *Bumper*
1897	*Grimalkan's* bill for *Feline Emancipation*.
1898	Debate in the *Damerfesk* on *Feline Emancipation*.
1898–1901	*Lord Big's* retirement to the *Tracities*.
1902	The *Princes* enter the *Royal Chessary*.
1903	Threat of war with *Prussia*.
1904	*Big* and the *Princes* in *Turkey*. Defeat of *War party*.
1905	*Exclusion Bill*.
1906	The *Princes* leave the *Royal Chessary*.
1908	Death of *Hawki IV* & *Benjamin VI*; accession of *Hawki V* & *Benjamin VII*.
1909	Coronation of *Hawki V* & *Benjamin VII*.
	Orring's League. *P. Green's* new *Clique* Bill.
	War with the *Tracity Islands*.

v *Geography*

While a simple criticism suffices to clear up the chronology of the Boxonian world, the same cannot be said for its geography. As regards the configuration of the principle land masses all the extant maps show a remarkable uniformity, but as regards the scale it is quite impossible to reconcile any of the maps with the distances implied in the texts where journies are described. Over the orientation insoluable problems arise, the climates and products of many countries being apparently incompatible with the latitudes to which all maps assign them. How far this puzzle could be solved by assuming for the axis of the Boxonian globe an angle different from the terrestrial, is a question which the present writer feels himself incompetent to discuss. He is therefore reluctantly compelled to leave the whole geographical problem to some future Boxonologist.